T0290265

Real Estate
———
A Love Story

Real Estate

A Love Story

WISDOM, HONOR, AND BEAUTY
IN THE TOUGHEST BUSINESS
IN THE WORLD

Joshua Benaim

DISRUPTION
BOOKS

New York Austin

Published by Disruption Books
New York, New York
www.disruptionbooks.com

Distributed by Disruption Books

For ordering information or special discounts for bulk purchases, please contact Disruption Books at info@disruptionbooks.com.

Library of Congress Control Number: 2021905047

Cover photograph by Joshua Benaim: The MBA Class of 1959 Chapel,
Harvard Business School; Moshe Safdie and Associates, architects

Cover design by David Gee
Text design by Brian Phillips Design

ISBN: 978-1-63331-053-7

Ebook ISBN: 978-1-63331-056-8

First Edition

For my children, Raphael, Lila, and Elijah

Contents

Preface

This is a love story about real estate investment and development, illustrated through my life experiences. It's a tale of the constant struggle between bravery and prudence, between the desire to create great things and add to the fabric of our cities, and the patience to choose the right time and circumstances to invest. It's a story of the power of a small gesture to transform a space, or a life. It is the saga of building great buildings that are well used and well loved, and perhaps, if you're lucky, leaving a small corner of the earth in better shape than when you found it.

The real estate world that I love is a world of ideas and inspiration, filled with the excitement of enterprise. Making a life in real estate means cutting your own path through an international maelstrom of idiosyncratic characters—scoundrels, craftsmen, visionaries, financiers, charlatans, traders, and thieves. On a typical day, I might spend hours brainstorming or negotiating with Greeks and Turks, Chinese and Russians, Israelis and Arabs, Mexicans, French, Ethiopians, Koreans, Persians, Brazilians, and Americans from all corners of our beautiful country . . . sometimes simultaneously! Navigating the dynamic world of real estate as a person of conscience takes hard work and constant learning. The reward is the characters you meet that dance to their own special music. You get the chance to learn from them how to make work meaningful and fulfilling.

In 2009, amidst the worst financial crisis in a generation, I left the certainty of my job and set out to hew my own path in the field. I had a few ideas on how I wanted to practice real estate, and I decided to try them out. In particular, I felt that a combination of a value investment philosophy with traditional real estate principles could lead to great results, without incurring great risk. I wanted to start a company grounded in my own ethos, judgment, and honorable way of treating people. I wondered whether there was a way to make great buildings despite my innate caution and risk aversion. Could my abstract principles lead to financial successes, or would I be eaten alive by the rough and tumble of real estate's daily challenges, frequent depredations, and constant negotiations?

I decided to write this book to distill my thoughts on the marriage of a value investment philosophy with traditional real estate principles, the idea that led me to start my company, Aria. But the more I thought about it, I realized that what I had discovered through experience could only be transmitted through stories and the people who had brought those stories to life. So I've included some personal stories from my career in real estate, as well as legends from my heroes and mentors, to illustrate those principles.

Part I recounts how I fell in love with the real estate business. Over the years, I've found that I approach real estate investment and development quite differently from most people I've met. Parts II and III offer my two cents on those two great disciplines, interspersed with my thoughts on how I feel business can and should be done. When Covid took the world by storm and upended our industry, I added a Part IV to explore the impact of technological changes on real estate, and to share some thoughts on the urgent task of bringing back our great cities.

We are living in a moment when moral leadership is scarce. Trust is eroding, and our country is divided. The reputation of the industry I love in the country I love is under threat. We desperately need a positive vision for business. I believe there is a different way to do business, one that aspires to higher ideals. One that is smart and fun and profitable, and also thoughtful and soulful.

I hope you will enjoy reading this book and that your curiosity will be piqued. These are my most precious lessons from business and life. At best, they may provide some guidance in building a meaningful career in the business world. If by chance you are also in the real estate business, I may have divulged too much! Please promptly forget all the strategies and tricks of the trade in a wine-induced siesta. But enjoy the philosophical parts.

Constant learning and self-improvement are vital to any great enterprise. I hope you will think of improvements and refinements to these ideas, share them with me, and proceed to use them for good.

New York, March 2019

PART I

How I Fell in Love with Real Estate

Kismet

I grew up in New York City in the 1970s and 1980s. I was really supposed to be a philosopher or a professor. I was a voracious reader and devoured any book I could get my hands on, from history to mythology to Encyclopedia Brown. I grew up collecting baseball cards, watching *Sesame Street*, and living the agony and the ecstasy of the '86 Mets. I loved climbing a big magnolia tree in my grandfather's backyard and playing Ping-Pong on an improvised table made of plumbing pipes and painted plywood. I enjoyed watching *Star Wars* and *Indiana Jones* for the umpteenth time with homemade popcorn. I wore big glasses that won me a lot of ribbing as a kid, until I learned to stick up for myself. I was a dreamer, an outsider, and a thinker.

Growing up on the West Side of Manhattan, pretzel vendors, yellow checker cabs, and feeding pigeons in Central Park were my daily fare. I lived in a neighborhood filled with fascinating people pursuing their dreams. One day on the way home from school, while waiting in the drizzle for an M10 bus that wouldn't show up, I offered to share a taxi with a lady who was going the same way with a stroller and a young boy. Everyone shared cabs back then (if you could afford to take one), and you'd usually get a good story in the bargain. It turned out she studied opera, and she offered to take me with her to her lesson. She mentioned something about *kismet*, which she explained was Turkish for "serendipity." It seemed safe enough, so I decided to tag along. That was how I began singing opera. Maybe that taxi ride was meant to be. It was certainly a chance encounter that changed my life.

We met Sam Sakarian, a Detroit-born tenor who gave up a career as a baseball player and his job as a foreman at the local Ford plant to pursue opera after coming back from World War II. Sam initiated me into the Italian school of *bel canto*, or "beautiful singing." It was a great tradition, passed on from generation to generation of opera singers, that aspired to make every phrase beautiful and meaningful. Sam used to point to his chest and say that the correct placement of the voice is through the heart. From him I learned another way to engage with the world, one filled with arcane knowledge, tradition, emotion, and beauty. I have the magic of New York to thank for such good luck.

I loved collecting stamps as a kid. My father and I would soak envelopes in water to loosen the glue. Then we'd dry the stamps and flatten them under a large dictionary. The letters poured in. My family had been scattered all around the world by the various calamities that befell the Jewish people during the twentieth century. My family's stories and legends left an indelible mark on my outlook. They emphasized doing the right thing and cultivating your mind. That's all you can count on when you're forced to flee.

In one corner of our apartment there was a wooden chest that was over a hundred years old. As a kid, I thought it was a treasure chest. It belonged to one of our ancestors who had left Spanish Morocco at the age of thirteen to seek his fortune in the rubber plantations of the Amazon. One night he heard the sound of a baby crying outside his hut. He started to go out to help when he learned it was the cry of an alligator!

I could not have been more lucky to be born in the family or city or country that I love. My parents are incredibly loving, kind, and thoughtful. And I grew up in an incredible extended family full of unique characters, brothers, mentors, thinkers, adventurers, inventors, and friends.

In each country where my family lived there were centuries of oppression punctuated by windows of flourishing, much like Mark Twain's quip that Wagner operas have wonderful moments, and dreadful quarter hours. In Spain, my ancestors experienced the great medieval *convivencia* of Jews, Moslems, and Christians and a flourishing of knowledge, philosophy, and humanities. Ferdinand and Isabella put an end to that with the Edict of Expulsion in 1492, and my father's family headed across the Straits of Gibraltar to northern Morocco.

One day while my father Carlos was studying in France, my grandmother Raquel heard banging on the door. It was the military police. We will never know exactly what happened that day, but the die was cast. My grandfather wrote a cryptic letter to my father, using the medieval Judeo-Spanish language for fear of it being opened by military censors, encouraging him to "spend the holiday with his uncle in the Canary Islands." With that, my father's idyllic youth in the seaside international city of Tangier, and ultimately my family's five-hundred-year presence in northern Morocco, came to an end. My dad came to America in 1969, where he met my mom and decided to stay and make a family with her in New York. And that's how I got lucky enough to be born in America and in New York City.

My mother, Darel, grew up in Hartsdale, New York, and became a psychologist and psychoanalyst while putting her heart and soul into raising three boys. She was a terrific mom. I truly admire her empathy and idealism, not to mention her stamina and dedication in putting up with us!

We were a close family, and my mother's parents were a huge presence in my childhood. They met in New York in the 1940s. Bernice was from Brooklyn. Eskandar was from Persia. He spoke English with a French accent, which is partly why she fell for him.

The story goes that he was looking for a bookkeeper and put an ad in the paper for a "librarian." This story is almost certainly not true.

Her family was from a town in Central Europe that changed from Austria to Russia to Poland depending on the day. Emperor Franz Josef was celebrated by my great-grandmother, but the Cossacks were dreaded. Ultimately, Nazism led to annihilation for those who remained. In the Persia of my grandfather, the Pahlavi Shahs let my family breathe, while the fanatical mullahs of the nineteenth century and Khomeini and Islamic fundamentalism in the twentieth not at all. Growing up, all of this history was still very fresh in our memory.

I was surrounded by people living an old-world life in many different tribes. I was amazingly lucky to be welcomed into the world of these cultures with love. I was squeezed tight with terms of endearment from the far corners of the world in English, Spanish, French, Persian, Arabic, Hebrew, and Yiddish. I recently tried to figure out what some of these phrases mean, in case I want to use them with my own kids. I learned that one directly translated means "Thanks be to God, I would walk circles around your head!" You get the picture. As a kid, I had to find a way to communicate with these wonderful characters and unlock the meaning of my family stories. Immersing myself in languages, cultures, and history has brought me immense joy and intellectual growth to this day.

My family's stories also brought into relief just how special America is in human history. How lucky we were to live in a free country founded on ideals! One that tried to do better and right itself when it went astray. America opened its arms to my parents and grandparents, gave them hope and the opportunity to build a good life. A festive Thanksgiving morning complete with bagels and lox became a family tradition, animated by the joyful spirit of the Thanksgiving parade that ran right through our neighborhood.

The legends of my family gave me the values that I aspire to live by. These values are rare, and in my view, worth preserving. Real estate offered me the chance to try to live by them. Wisdom, honor, learning, thrift, passion—each found its place in my love affair with the real estate business.

Wisdom

When I think about how my life ended up the way it has, and how I see life and business, I am immediately drawn to memories of my grandfather Eskandar, or Mr. E as he was known in the business world. His love and wisdom were beacons throughout my life.

He arrived in the United States in 1941 from Persia on a Dutch ship that took 113 days to cross the Pacific. During the journey he refused to spend ten cents to buy a Coke like the American sailors on board. He was saving his dimes for telegrams to his mother. My grandfather came to America to find opportunity. And also to chauffeur his newly married brother on his honeymoon to Niagara Falls.

Growing up in a mud house in Persia, his first experience in real estate was collecting old bricks from a demolition site in a wheelbarrow to reuse them in new construction. He then traveled the bazaars and marketplaces of the Middle East and Europe trading antiques. He spent his first years in the U.S. driving up and down the Eastern seaboard, carefully wrapping his antiques in newspaper each evening, and then unwrapping them in the next city the following morning.

Mr. E brought his deeply held values to the real estate business. He had graduated from the School of Hard Knocks. He hated waste and loved a bargain. He valued beautiful old buildings and put them to good use in the same way he would spend hours repairing broken pottery by hand. He was personally involved, and his word was his bond.

Mr. E appreciated a great location. Family lore has it that when their father saw Mr. E and his brothers off to New York City, he advised them to one day buy something near the Empire State Building, where Rockefeller was building the tallest building in the world. Twenty years of hard work later, Mr. E bought his first building. He told me that he was so afraid of making a mistake that he went back to the seller and begged him to give him back his deposit. Then he girded up his courage and bought another one.

Mr. E knew the difference between authenticity and "junk." In his eyes, old and rare was more precious than new and disposable. He negotiated prices and kept an eye out for charlatans. He had an artist's eye and even tried his hand at painting. But his most fantastic creations were the chandeliers and candelabras he crafted from salvaged prisms of Bohemian crystal.

I would often be seen by his side as a kid. I even lost my first tooth at my grandfather's house. Mr. E lived in a big house with his brothers and their mother. They raised their families in a kind of old-world compound surrounded by Romantic English gardens where they would sip tea and play backgammon. At the center of this cascading landscape was my grandfather, Mr. E. He would be in an undershirt, standing over a pot of Persian rice, humming a classic American song like "Home on the Range." He loved America. Into his eighties you would not believe the childlike delight the poor boy from the desert found in opening a particularly ripe melon.

Mr. E hated risk, and he was an incredibly cautious investor. But at the same time, he was an adventurer who left his country to try his luck in the United States, in New York City. It was a paradox that I returned to continuously in my search to do real estate in a meaningful way. He combined thrift and stoicism with entrepreneurial energy. Despite his risk aversion, with great patience, he managed to build important high-rise buildings in Manhattan and a terrific family.

Traditional real estate combines a value orientation with a love

REAL ESTATE, A LOVE STORY

of land, buildings, and great cities. It inspires you to create something lasting and useful, while making a wise and prudent investment. It requires you to engage personally with the marketplace, with the city, and with workmen, neighbors, activists, and partners as a whole person of integrity. There are many ways to do business. This is one that I find especially honorable and that has been demonstrably rewarding. The wisdom of Mr. E, his love, and his patience have been guiding lights in making my career in business, and they animate many of the stories in this book.

Value

When I decided to start my company in real estate, I found inspiration in Mr. E's love of old-world charm and his patience in repairing antiques. He could spend hours hunched over the kitchen counter deep in concentration, carefully putting each piece of an antique Chinese vase into place with plaster of Paris. Perhaps the vase had been excavated in pieces, or perhaps it had broken on the journey. Either way he was getting a bargain by buying a box full of porcelain shards. After months of patiently putting the pieces together, a beautiful and precious vase would emerge.

Many years later, as I set out to start my own business, I resolved to keep an eye out for shards of pottery that might be repaired into something whole and special. An opportunity came sooner than I anticipated. I opened an email offering a fantastic apartment building in the West Village of Manhattan. It was a "50-footer," in the lingo of New York real estate, where tenements or lots are classified by their width. When the street grid of New York City was drawn up in the nineteenth century, land was parceled out in 25 x 100-foot lots, and most buildings from that vintage are built on multiples of those original lots. The building was located on a charming, tree-lined stretch of Bank Street around the corner from the newly famous Magnolia Bakery. As I scanned the offering sheet, one detail jumped out at me. What was for sale was not the entire building, it was a 52 percent tenants-in-common interest.

Tenants-in-common ownership is an archaic form of land ownership originally derived from English Common Law. It is governed by a code of tradition and precedents rooted in the Middle Ages. Each party has equal control of the property, irrespective of percentage ownership. It's not based on voting rights; you're practically joined at the hip! It survives today in some obscure property deals and in one other place—it's how husbands and wives automatically hold property together.

Sharing a building with an unknown partner—through an arcane structure tantamount to owning marital property—was pretty daunting! Most people advised me to steer clear of such a headache. It was certainly enough to deter most real estate investors from considering the deal. But I was intrigued. I liked the intellectual challenge of figuring out an obscure, historical legal structure. Perhaps this handsome building was a beautiful vase that just needed someone to put its pieces back together.

I had to do some excavating to find the missing pieces. Who was the mysterious 48 percent owner? No one would say. The seller wanted to make a quick binding deal to reinvest the proceeds in a project in Greece, leaving us in bed with a stranger. Once we had shaken hands on the deal, I met the 48 percent owner at an Upper East Side diner. The much-feared tenant-in-common turned out to be a lovely older lady who had come from Japan as a young woman engaged to an American serviceman. She was eminently reasonable and a pleasure to work with. She decided to sell half of her interest to us and keep half so her children could benefit from our hard work over the years.

Upon closer examination, it turned out that the property wasn't held as tenants-in-common at all. It was a general partnership, another archaic structure. We resolved to convert it into a garden-variety Limited Liability Company with a proper operating agreement rather than relying upon arcane court precedents. This made the property more liquid and financeable.

Then we rolled up our sleeves and upgraded apartments that hadn't been touched since at least the 1950s. We added a laundry room and a video intercom system. We even found some extra bedrooms by building contemporary open kitchens and recapturing the former ones as bedrooms. In the aftermath of the Great Recession, having roommates was a great way to survive in the big city, and those extra bedrooms helped. Today the property is flourishing and fully occupied. It's in a great location in the West Village. Down the street, townhomes trade for many times the price of the building. Absent the complexities of the deal and our willingness to be contrarian, this property would have cost a fortune, and we would have missed out. By unifying a fragmented ownership structure and eschewing the easy route, a beautiful vase had begun to emerge from the pieces.

Investment

I remember the moment when I realized that the worldview I had inherited from my grandfather could be applied to business in a way that I believed in. The moment when I found a way to have conviction and act decisively while still being risk-averse, like my grandfather hunting for great antiquarian finds in the bazaar. It was when I spent twenty hours interviewing for a job with one of the great value investors of our time, Seth Klarman, and his colleagues at The Baupost Group.

My conversations with Seth opened my eyes to the discipline of investing. They set me on a path of discovery in the pursuit of value investment in real estate. My business school real estate professor Arthur Segel introduced me to Seth because, to my amazement, he thought I had the chops to work with one of the great investors of our day. Baupost has assembled an incredible track record since its founding in 1982.

Seth asked the most probing and intellectually rigorous questions I've ever encountered in an interview. He opened with, "What is in your soul?" and delved deeper from there! I really had to think about that one. My family, friends, music, faith, intellectual enterprise, and aspirations to make the world a better place were up there. Business certainly had a place too, especially finding bargains, putting puzzle pieces together, and making buildings that were useful, beautiful, and profitable.

What I gleaned from my discussions with Seth was both a set of principles and an ethos of investing that resonated deeply with me. The philosophy of value investing is one of patiently searching for special opportunities that others miss. It's built on an ingrained risk aversion that helps avoid catastrophic losses, which often end the careers of the flashy and impetuous. A willingness to buck the crowd has been with me from my childhood. I was content with my big glasses and reading books, having a few great friends, and playing backgammon with my grandfather. This philosophy made sense to me.

The principles of value investing are deceptively simple. Value investment is the discipline of buying good assets for less than their intrinsic worth. It has been described as buying a dollar for fifty cents. While it sounds straightforward, it's pretty tough to put into practice. How do you find situations where you can buy things for less than they're worth? After all, you wouldn't go into a self-respecting pizzeria in New York and ask for a slice at half price. Half a token won't get you on the subway. Forgive the dated reference from my youth in New York City—with MetroCards, even a whole token won't get you very far!

The answer—what I most love about value investment in real estate—is that you have to use your brain. You have to wade through all the complexity to find broken pieces and make them whole. I love the intellectual rigor of value investment. It is not a domain for the competitive gunslingers of finance. Value investment favors the intellectual seekers, the curious, and the patient. It's the world of Benjamin Graham, who balanced investing with a Columbia professorship, and Warren Buffett, who reads a book a day to keep his mind sharp. He still lives in the Omaha home he started out in.

Value investors are a rugged band of contrarians and misfits. They make a living on brainpower and elbow grease. They have to weather the scorn of the trendy and popular until their wisdom prevails, usually in a downturn. All of their theories are written in books that few people bother to read. Their ethos combines confidence with humility, as their quest to buy below value leaves room for human error. This is the place in business where I found my "tribe." It appealed to the archaeologist in me, the chess player, the stamp collector, and the book lover. This worldview is deeply connected to the way of life I learned from Mr. E.

Value investment also resonated with my quest to seize opportunities in life without taking on too much risk. Risk can be avoided by paying less for an asset. When one focuses on the downside of the investment, and buys something great cheap, the upside often takes care of itself. This was a revelation to me. It offered the freedom to do exciting things in the world without too much fear. You can manage the risk of investing by buying assets that are misunderstood or out of favor, and that the market consequently values below their intrinsic worth. You can see through the dust and grime on the shards of pottery and recognize the value in them.

I don't like risk. I'm just not comfortable with much of it. Perhaps this comes from my family. Mr. E is apocryphally known to have warned of the dangerous undertow—in a lake! Family stories of risk conjured images of the mullahs taking over, women dirtying their faces with charcoal to escape the attention of marauding Cossacks, and corrupt Argentine policemen demanding protection money.

I had to find a way to embrace business despite the many risks around us. A lot of business is about trying to predict the future, understanding where people will be in five, ten, twenty years. But the future is unpredictable. If you're wrong, you will lose a lot of money and time. I love history. I prefer to predict the past. As a value investor, you can have the luxury of making bets that don't principally depend on where the world is going. You can do just fine if the world stays the same.

You can even make investments that will be okay if the world gets a little worse. That cushion is called a "margin of safety" and is much prized by value investors. Seth Klarman wrote a great book called *Margin of Safety*, which lays out his risk-averse approach to finding value. Thank goodness not too many people have the patience to read it, or many of the bargains would disappear!

Most value investment lore is focused on the stock and bond markets, securities of public companies where epic fortunes have been made or lost. Struck by Seth's observations and their resonance with the wisdom of Mr. E, I decided to see how I could apply value investment to real estate. These two sources of strength and guidance have given me the courage to invest and build my own business.

Why is value investment so important to me? I can afford some indulgences at this point and could afford to invest more aggressively. But I don't. I've often felt like my life was lived in reverse, that as a boy I had the ethos of an old man, and it's taken me over forty years to learn to grow into a young man at heart.

Intellect

I started to see the broken vase everywhere I looked. The world of real estate was filled with beautiful pottery that was in pieces. I saw it in the defaulted mortgage on a half-built building in Little Havana in Miami. It was advertised as 95 percent complete, but we soon realized that was a mirage. It was a twelve-story elevator building with a hundred-car garage. We were able to buy the note from the bank for fifty cents on the dollar because the capital structure was broken and the asset itself was incomplete.

I saw the broken vase in buying all the condominium units in a building in Miami to free up the land for development. Then we tried the same thing in DC. We were negotiating to buy twenty-seven units in a rare fifty-two-unit apartment building in Foggy Bottom, near the State Department and George Washington University. Almost all the property in that neighborhood is held by institutions. There was a lot of demand for housing and very little supply. During the negotiations, the broker managed to assemble forty-one of the units. Then we met with a doctor who owned two more, and he agreed to give us a lease with the option to buy. In the successive years we got one more. The broken vase school of real estate rewards patience.

The broken vase was the theme behind buying a property in New York where the gas had been shut down in the winter. It was also manifested in buying a magnificent parcel of oceanfront land in Florida that was leased for many years for zero return. In 1955, the landowner had leased the land to a developer at what was then the market price of $6,000 per year, without taking into account inflation. To make matters worse, or more broken, the underlying land was owned in a partnership of a brother and a sister who were in litigation and not on speaking terms. Each sibling was fine with selling to us at a reasonable price, so long as the dastardly other sibling didn't get a penny more. We bought the partnership interests in the land encumbered by that lease with the hope of reuniting it with the leasehold interest. In that deal, the vase will fix itself when the lease expires. The passage of time is the only catalyst needed to realize a great return.

I even saw the broken vase in the Colony Beach and Tennis Resort, where the condo association had filed for bankruptcy. The Colony was a beautiful resort that embraced "casual elegance" on Longboat Key in Sarasota, Florida. I had been there as a kid, and later sang there. You stayed in low-key bungalows, but the tennis program was incredible and the ocean was spectacular.

The complexity of the deal structure was unparalleled. The land was divided into two parcels, one with the tennis courts and the pool, another with 237 condominium units governed by a condo board that had gone rogue. The condo unit owners were also limited partners in a partnership that operated the resort as a hotel. The general partner was engaged in a dispute with the board over the cost of maintaining the rustic chic units. Bank of America was selling the notes secured by the pool and tennis courts. I decided against buying them even though I saw some easy win-wins. I didn't want to have to argue with 237 condo owners over access to their tennis courts!

But I did buy two units for $120,000 with my savings from my job in finance, with the hope of crashing in my bohemian paradise on the beach. Instead I got a crash course in real estate law. I learned the lesson that repairing the broken vase is sometimes a lot more complicated than it looks. To paraphrase John Maynard Keynes, a condo board can stay irrational longer than you can remain solvent.

I was lucky to get out with my shirt. That vase stayed broken. It's only now starting to be put back together. P.S. It's still in litigation some ten years later, and I never got to set foot in the units!

I was pretty excited to be finding the keys to unlocking value in real estate. If I was willing to embrace complexity, and use my noggin, there weren't many others who would tread where I could go. It enabled me to buy great assets cheaply, and therefore safely. Deals could be fragmented in time, space, partnership, or debt structure. The best deals were cases where the finances were broken *and* the asset itself needed repair. It took an investor who was willing to roll up his sleeves and get the job done. The broken vase was restored when the capital structure was healed with more equity, and we finished the building with a lot of care and attention.

Reuniting fragmented ownership structures became my watchword. In a sense, real estate was a gigantic puzzle. Finding bargains was possible, with patience and the right thinking. It was the value investment of Seth Klarman applied to real estate, with a dash of Mr. E's wisdom to seal the deal. And it rewarded those who looked at things differently and found unappreciated assets. As an outsider growing up, I knew in my bones that value could be found in something unappreciated. And I loved that I had found a place to use my brains to make money and avoid risk.

The broken vase was my key to value investment in real estate. I had found a way to make business meaningful and challenging and profitable. And I thought it would be my only method. Until I discovered other tools to make business successful and meaningful that came from deep in my past.

Passion

You might ask yourself how someone who doesn't like risk ended up doing real estate. When I look back at what would inspire my career in the real estate business, a big part of the answer is opera. That's where the entrepreneurial piece of my story came from.

After the fateful cab ride, opera became an exciting part of my life. I learned arias and duets, listened to scratchy old recordings, and discovered the great singers of the past. I sat with the libretto while listening to operas so I could understand what the words meant. Opera was filled with passionate characters and great stories. As an undergraduate at Harvard, I feasted on social studies and philosophy during the day. I sang my heart out at night. I got to sing Italian love songs, Argentine tangos, Mozart, and Beethoven.

At my first job after college at Credit Suisse First Boston, I also sang—on the rare occasions I could sneak away from my desk. My venue of choice was the elevator machine room on the top floor. There I could sing loud and clear, and no one downstairs could really hear! My biggest fans were Latino maintenance men, who loved my operatic renditions and Spanish love songs.

Many of the word processors and graphic designers at the bank were struggling actors and opera singers trying to make it in New York. Sometimes I felt I had more in common with them than with the bankers. But I was scared as hell of a life in opera and the possibility that without a more established career I would be lost. I remember when a couple of my opera singer friends got married in their apartment. Instead of wedding presents, they joked that they were registered with Con Edison.

In my early twenties, I threw myself into opera with all I had. I honestly felt as if I had walked off a cliff. I had grown accustomed to a comfortable set of boundaries working in investment banking. I liked my desk. I even looked forward to going into the office on weekends in my sneakers (I didn't have much of a choice about the weekend thing). My job offered a clear career path, which appealed to my risk aversion. Opera had none of that certainty. I was completely out of my element on stage, playing a medieval warrior king one day, a bohemian Parisian painter the next. Yet this impossible challenge became a tremendous source of motivation. With nothing to lose but my pride, I dove in headfirst.

My first job in opera was an apprenticeship with the Sarasota Opera. I auditioned for the company in my final days of investment banking and got the job. I had to memorize four opera chorus parts, which was pretty challenging. They were the *Der Fliegende Hollander* (German), *Les Pêcheurs de Perles* (French), *Il Barbiere di Siviglia*, and *Alzira* (both Italian). While I studied the music I needed to learn for my apprenticeship, I earned a few bucks setting up valuation models for the first REIT (Real Estate Investment Trust) hedge fund, Highrise Partners, at the request of my old boss, Dean. Dean was a jazz musician and a deal-making genius. He wanted to apply a rigorous valuation process to the real estate assets that comprised the trusts, which was a great exercise in applying the corporate finance of mergers and acquisitions to real estate in all its shapes and forms.

My job in Sarasota finally rolled around. I packed my bags and went to learn how to perform opera. It was there that I met the conductor Victor DeRenzi, known within the company as "The Maestro." The Maestro believes deeply in the power of opera to connect us to our humanity. For him, music is not mere entertainment, but a call to be our better selves. His hero is the great Italian composer Giuseppe Verdi. Each year, on the anniversary of Verdi's death, he leads the entire opera company in singing "Va pensiero," or the "Chorus of the Hebrew Slaves" in *Nabucco* that became a heartfelt anthem of freedom and humanity.

The Maestro makes great music according to deeply held beliefs. He passed over many professional opportunities because he wouldn't compromise in honoring the intentions of the opera's composer. The Maestro shares the value investor's disdain for popular fads, along with a willingness to hew his own path through the professional world according to fixed principles. He is an idealist and has very high standards. Working with the Maestro showed me the importance of standing up with the courage of your convictions. He believed in me and became an important mentor.

Opera has of late been poisoned by vulgar modern reinterpretations passing as high art. These shallow, narcissistic directorial caprices are disconnected from the authentic meaning of the words and the music. The Maestro has held his ground, eschewing any involvement with these fads and making his company a temple to authentic opera. This has cost him a lot of opportunities, but he has stuck to his guns. Doing something you believe in is a powerful way to go through life. It's not easy. But I believe it can be done in the business world too.

Opera

For several years, I traveled the United States playing the equivalent of AAA baseball. I sang *Madama Butterfly* in downtown Peoria, *La Bohème* in Silicon Valley and Central City, Colorado, and *The Barber of Seville* in the Bronx. I apprenticed amidst the exquisite rose-hued mesas of Santa Fe, New Mexico. I loved the landscape of cacti and pine trees and adobe homes. From the open-air opera house you could see a thunderstorm arriving from miles away.

Life in opera wasn't easy. Every few months you had to decamp and show up in a new place ready to make music. But I made friends with the other singers. I joined the YMCA, I met locals who showed me around. I got to experience other lifestyles and connect with other Americans who were pursuing their dreams or just getting by.

Singing a three- or four-hour opera on stage is an incredible challenge—physically, mentally, and emotionally. You have to be in tip-top shape, your voice has to project over an orchestra of fifty or sixty instruments, and you have to dominate the stage. You have to act the part with passion and commune with the audience.

It is the joy of rehearsing with the other singers, often exuberant, joyful people, that makes it worth it. The sound of a great orchestra with an inspired conductor is thrilling. When you go out on stage and the room is dark and there's a little circle of light that you have to stay in, the music gives you strength that you didn't know you had. You are in a sense an instrument of the music and the words, a vessel through which the meaning of the piece is communicated. That is an unbelievable high that lasts for hours after the performance.

In 2003, the Maestro gave me an incredible opportunity, one

of the principal roles in a rarely performed Italian opera called *The Love of Three Kings*. The play is set in the Dark Ages during the barbarian conquest of Italy. It has an exquisite orchestration, infused with some of the best elements of Italian, German, and French opera.

The story is centered around a love triangle. My character, the son of the blind barbarian king, loves his Italian bride, but she has never given up her princely Italian lover. My character plays a young idealistic man and a reluctant warrior. I truly love my wife and don't understand why she cannot reciprocate.

When my blind father catches my bride in the heat of passion with her old lover, he strangles her to death on stage. He then sets a trap by poisoning her lips while she lies in church, hoping to lure her secret lover to his death. Heartbroken, I kiss her lips and die in my father's arms. It was the height of my opera career. The chance to die on stage fulfilled my aspirations for meaning and passion in opera.

I want to do real estate the way the Maestro does opera. To make great investments and build great buildings based on conviction and a set of deeply held principles. It's not quite as visceral in real estate because you aren't the product. You create something beyond yourself that you put a lot of passion into, like a beautiful apartment building or meaningful changes in people's lives or an honorable reputation. It can be equally intense. The world of loyalty and betrayal, love and revenge, could just as easily describe real estate as opera! In opera, I got to step into the shoes of those great characters and stretch my personal range and repertoire. In real estate, I have tried to take on the mantle of some of my heroes and mentors.

In many ways I found the guts to do real estate in opera. On stage there is no equivocation. You have only a moment to take charge of the music and the character and make a statement, or be forgotten forever. I took from opera and working with the Maestro the belief that if you are doing something you believe in, seize the moment. Don't let a fundamental risk aversion paralyze you. Take action. In the case of value investment, if you've done your analysis and you believe in an investment and the downside risk is limited, go for it.

While value investment resonates deeply with who I am, I also want to bring passion and joy and emotion to what I do. Part of my journey has been reconciling these important roles, the opera singer and the intellectual and the businessman. I've come to accept some risk in the world.

I have also learned to bring some of the joy and adventure I found in opera to real estate development. I love the ability to bring beautiful buildings to life. I've learned to appreciate the architect's discipline of imbuing the functional necessities of living with some of the inherent beauty of nature, light, and history.

Opera survives on inspiration. It is possible to tap into this in real estate too, whether in the beauty of a project or in the constant array of human relations that characterizes the real estate arena. Seeking beauty, kindness, or grace in the practice of one's profession is not off limits. Real estate provides a surprisingly broad stage on which to practice the art of humanity.

Tradition

I first fell in love with real estate development in a moment of personal crisis. I had just come back to New York after a tour of Europe auditioning for operatic roles. I had lugged my suitcase from youth hostel to youth hostel, auditioning in smaller theaters in Europe. Months before, I had written letters to the theater directors requesting appointments. I didn't realize that it would be a lot easier to work with an agent to make all this happen. I thought I could do it myself and hit the road.

I think it was when I was in Barcelona staying at a religious hostel without air conditioning for thirty euros per night, feeling great pride at economizing, when I realized I was alone. I had traveled to Italy for auditions and visited Verona, the scene of Shakespeare's *Romeo and Juliet*. Looking up at Juliet's balcony, I knew that something was missing. A life in singing required tremendous sacrifices and loneliness, along with constant travel. I didn't think I wanted to do it. It was incredibly challenging professionally not to be able to be the best I could be at all times. Many of my auditions were unsuccessful and didn't make a significant impression. I felt like I had failed.

By the time I got an email at an internet cafe offering me a job covering a Verdi role at the famed Teatro Liceu of Barcelona, I had already made up my mind to find a new path. It was a pretty unsettling time for me. I had lost my grandfather, the Mr. E of many of the stories in this book, in 1999. Then, in 2001, September 11 had shattered the heart of the city I love. Like other New Yorkers, I went across town looking for loved ones. Not a lot was certain in that world. I had traveled the country singing opera and working in theaters, but I didn't have a fixed reference point or a professional home.

I plotted my next steps. I got a book on historic decisions of the Supreme Court from an English-language bookstore to get excited about a career in law. When I returned to New York, I decided to apply to law school while working for the next year. Just in case, I prepared applications for both law school and business school to see where I'd be accepted. Something told me that while law would satisfy my intellectual curiosity and give me the certainty of a good job, I might end up alone at the library, missing out on the richness of human experience.

To my surprise, I found that opera had liberated me from many of my worries about business. Failure? What better preparation than being vulnerable in a dark theater expressing extreme emotions in front of thousands of people! I found some career guidance in a book by a business school professor that really resonated with me. She posited that contrary to the conventional wisdom, finding one's true career calling did not come by searching within. No amount of introspection would reveal a hidden box with the answer. The answer lay outside the self in one's interaction with the world. Action was the key to self-discovery in business.

During this period, I had a chance to spend some time with my uncles, who were grappling with a development on William Street in Lower Manhattan. I was immediately intrigued by the chance to work with Jeffrey and Donald, who had pioneered great adaptations of historic buildings in New York City starting in the 1970s. Working with energetic family partners, including my cousins Alan and Robert, they converted ornate nineteenth-century warehouses into apartments that fit the needs of young professionals moving back into New York City.

They also found time to inculcate in me some of the most important lessons of young adulthood. Jeffrey has a zest for life and a love of music. He is the one who introduced me to opera as a teenager. Donald is a cowboy philosopher with a big heart. He is a Houdini at making the most out of small spaces. They also love to joke around. When I was a kid, they tried to convince me that there was an operation called a "tickle-ectomy" that would cure me from being ticklish forever—provided I submit to the imaginary procedure of sustained tickling! As an adult, Jeffrey and Donald showed unbelievable love and generosity in mentoring me in this business.

William Street was a good site for a high-rise apartment building, which my family had not constructed since the 1980s. When my grandfather and his brothers built buildings in the 1960s, 1970s, and 1980s, it was all hands on deck, with everyone in the family chipping in. The William Street partnership had the additional appeal of including Mr. E's brothers, my uncle Fred and uncle Henry, and their children. They were incredible builders and businessmen.

I took out my laptop and volunteered to help. My uncle Fred and his brothers had bought William Street in 1995 for a song. But the Financial District in Lower Manhattan had been dying a slow death, and September 11 in the neighborhood had frightened the hell out of everyone. The United States government passed the Liberty Bond bill to help rebuild Lower Manhattan in the wake of the devastation. My uncles and cousins were considering using the Liberty Bond financing to construct a rental apartment building.

In 2003, the nation was in recession for the second time in a short period. My first task was self-imposed—I wanted to understand the potential of the property in light of different risks. An erosion of rents was not implausible. In those days, the fortunes of the area around Wall Street were closely tied to the stock market.

To add to that, terrorism was on everyone's mind. The property was only a few blocks from the remains of the World Trade Center.

Liberty Bonds, which had been allocated by Congress to help rebuild Lower Manhattan, offered a powerful incentive. These were combined with tax-exempt bond financing administered by the state with tax abatements from the city. I ran the numbers on what kind of a hit the project could take if there was another terrorist attack, and probed other downside scenarios. It was the first time I was able to apply my techniques from finance and what I had learned from my uncles to understanding risk.

Archaeology

My father once returned from a trip to Egypt with several clay replica oil lamps. Knowing how much I loved the excitement of discovery and ancient Egyptian archaeology, my father and grandfather broke the lamps and buried the shards all around the garden. Then they gave me a shovel and invited me to an imaginary archaeological dig! I was to excavate the broken pieces and plaster them back together into finished ancient Egyptian oil lamps.

I really got hooked on real estate when we started with the geotechnical engineering studies that preceded excavation at William Street. It was right out of an archaeological dig. It turns out that there were dozens of pneumatic caissons buried below the surface of the site. What are pneumatic caissons? you may ask. According to a hundred-year-old news article that surfaced in a search of historic newspaper archives, pneumatic caissons were a miraculous structural invention of their time. They were essentially vacuum-pressured tubes, six or twelve feet in diameter, that were dug into the earth to keep the water out. Then they were filled with concrete all the way to bedrock three stories below the surface.

The article noted that a number of workmen had tragically met their end trying to install these massive airless structural elements. This was the same technology used to build the supports for the Brooklyn Bridge under the waters of the East River. Under normal conditions, it would take a lot of dynamite or heavy machinery to break up all that subsurface concrete. But that was not in the cards for these caissons. A brick subway tunnel constructed at the turn of the last century passed just a couple of feet from the property line.

We somehow had to remove gigantic concrete columns descending all the way to bedrock without disturbing the delicate antique subway tunnel just feet away. Any failure of the brick tunnel could cause catastrophic loss of life in the subway. So, working closely with the Metropolitan Transit Authority, we installed precision seismographic equipment in the tunnel. These readers had been created to detect the slightest earthquake activity. We pledged to conduct our excavation in such a way that the earthquake meters would rest undisturbed.

That was not all. The neighboring brick office building sat on wood piles. Given the amount of water that we believed was just below the surface, that posed a big problem. Wood piles that are constantly submerged in water like piers do not rot. Neither do dry piles. But piles that have been exposed to water and then become dry are primed for rotting. This meant that it was necessary to excavate while maintaining the hydrostatic pressure, the water pressure, of the neighboring property.

When you excavate and dewater a giant hole, it dramatically changes the water pressure around you, potentially destabilizing the neighbors and their submerged piles. For this reason, a slurry wall, or "bathtub," had to be created around the perimeter of the property to protect the neighbors during excavation. All of these factors combined to make this excavation, in the words of one engineer, akin to digging out the site with a teaspoon!

If we had to excavate several stories down, we might as well have a large underground garage. But I didn't anticipate this would take us on another adventure in architectural history. It turned out that our ability to retain a curb cut for cars to enter the garage rested on how long it had been there. To be legally grandfathered in, it had to have been in place prior to the adoption of the relevant code— some fifty years earlier! Finding out when the curb cut had come into existence meant poring over handwritten nineteenth-century records looking for easements or alleys. Given the time period, this could mean cars or horses and carriages!

A forensic architectural mystery was just what the doctor ordered. We engaged an architectural historian to review newspaper reports and other archival sources. The property was once the site of the Corn Exchange Bank, a proud commercial institution that over the years had been merged into Chemical Bank and then Chase Manhattan Bank and finally JPMorgan Chase. The building had been torn down during the real estate boom of the 1980s with the intention of constructing a brand-new office building on the site. Then came the stock market crash of 1987, changes to the tax laws, the savings and loan crisis, and the deep recession of the early 1990s. The site had been a parking lot for more than fifteen years.

We scoured the archives but didn't find anything relevant. Finally, one blurry photograph showed a man carrying a wheelbarrow into the building through what appeared to be a service entrance! This would have to suffice.

William Street also gave me my first taste of the art of floor plans. My cousin Jed and uncle Donald would confer on how best to lay out the apartments on a typical floor. They pored over the minutiae of where every closet and bathroom should go, which exposures should go to two bedrooms versus one bedrooms or studios, the number of each unit type per floor, and every other imaginable configuration. My uncle Donald has a special understanding of space. He is able to look at two-dimensional scale drawings and envision what the units would feel like. I have a really hard time grasping three-dimensional space. I was always more of a sound and smell and taste guy, less visual. But this experience showed me the power of floor plans to shape space, and also the profound impact of architectural space planning on economics and life.

Energized by the adventure of discovering structural engineering, architecture, and a visceral connection to the history of New York, I decided to go to business school to learn more. The prospect of developing William Street was very exciting, and I felt like I was connecting with my family history, and with potential teachers and mentors. In a strange way, I felt like I was communing with my grandfather Mr. E and immersing myself in his tradition. On top of that, the work involved intellectual puzzles, historical sleuthing, and a kind of hands-on archaeology that appealed to my brainy side.

To pass the time while waiting for school to start, I cut my teeth on the renovation of a lobby that needed updating. I learned the joys of renovation and hands-on work in the field. There were also moments of frustration, like the time I sent scale drawings to the contractor by fax. The plans arrived so distorted on the other side that the doors didn't fit! But I was hooked. I was on a new path of business and real estate and learning by doing.

Beauty

Beauty might seem more suited to a discussion of ancient Greek sculpture or English Romantic poetry, but it is an essential and underappreciated part of real estate. It's a fair goal as an end in itself, to add to the beauty of the world around us. But it is of economic value as well. In real estate, beauty can uplift us, make us feel at home, or invigorate us for a hard day's work. That's important to people, and even a hard-nosed businessman ignores it at his own peril.

For one thing, beauty doesn't have to be expensive. Beauty can come in the form of a ray of light in a room through a well-placed window, oriented toward the path of the sun. A cool breeze in the summer. A view of the horizon from high ground. Or the scent of jasmine in the evening. Each of which may be free.

Beauty can also be man-made, in the form of harmonious materials, historic stonework or details, or simplicity. Beauty affects how people feel when they enter a place, and that psychology affects demand. If it can be achieved at the right price, beauty can drive high returns.

One of my favorite examples of bringing out the beauty of an asset without enormous expenditure is The Bond apartments in Washington, DC. We acquired a vacant 1920s building in the West End near Dupont Circle from the International Monetary Fund. The building was used as extended-stay accommodations for student economists. Over time, the interiors had been altered and made the building feel like a transient, low-priced hotel, while the exterior and entrance had fallen into disrepair. When the IMF bought a 1960s apartment house next door, they combined the two buildings and closed up the entrance of The Bond.

Something about the building reminded me of many I had seen growing up in New York. All around the West Side were stately *grande dames* from the Gilded Age that had fallen into disrepair, conjuring the decaying grandeur of a lost golden age. In those days, the most prized buildings were termed "prewar," originally meaning built prior to World War I. During that fertile period in the growth of cities that included the invention of the elevator, the first modern apartment buildings were built. They were designed with an elegance and architectural idiom to evoke London or Paris on a larger scale. Then came the Great Depression and the Second World War and a couple of generations of much more frugal construction. Lower ceilings, less attention to detail, and a flight to the suburbs ensured that prewar buildings remained the undisputed champions of New York real estate until at least the 2000s.

The Bond felt like a partially carved slab of marble that with a few small gestures could be chiseled into a great sculpture. It wanted to be a grand prewar building that would be equally at home on Central Park West. But it needed some swift attention. Its architectural details were fairly cheap add-ons from the building boom of the Roaring Twenties. Every architect that I spoke to wanted to modernize the building with glass and steel. Modern Class A apartments were getting the highest rents in the District, and the natural move was to embrace modernity. Many nearby buildings had been reskinned, meaning that the traditional facades had been taken off and replaced with new, modern exteriors.

I took the road less traveled. I decided to try to create the grand building that The Bond had never quite been, with a few gestures that wouldn't break the bank. One of the features that distinguishes the best prewar buildings in New York is a cast-iron canopy. After traveling far and wide to photograph the most elegant canopies I could find, I settled on a design based on the Saks Fifth

Avenue canopy in New York. Poring over catalogues of antique metalwork details, I located the Utah company that had restored it. As luck would have it, they still had the molds! They cast the ornaments, and we saved money by assembling the frame at an industrial steelworks in Baltimore.

When the building opened, prospective residents were drawn to its grand presence on the street. Everyone thought that the canopy had been there forever. Tenants felt happy to walk home to something beautiful. It made living in a compact city apartment worth it.

A small gesture to bring out the beauty of a property had a meaningful impact on the rents. As a value investor, if I could increase returns by lavishing an asset with beauty, so much the better. But beyond that was another realization. The decision to create the canopy was rooted in my own idiosyncratic experiences on the West Side, my love of history, and my discovery of the Saks Fifth Avenue canopy molds. No other developer would have made the same choices. I got to buck the crowd and make the building beautiful in my own way. I discovered the exhilarating potential of creativity in real estate.

Architecture

Creating something beautiful that also had an immediate economic impact was a powerful experience. It brought people joy to walk into The Bond, much as it had brought joy when I sang in my previous life. There weren't a lot of ways to achieve that in business! I began to wonder if I could do it more often. I still wanted to buy things cheaply, and I could never knowingly overpay, but perhaps I could also make the buildings I bought more efficient and more beautiful.

A small gesture creating big meaning reminded me of a concept in opera used to great effect by the great Italian composer Giuseppe Verdi. His operas were meant for people of all classes and all walks of life, Italian peasants and gentry, and audiences around the world. I once sang at an opera house in Central City, Colorado, where a rugged band of Welsh miners had put on their own production of Verdi's *Il Trovatore* in the 1850s.

Verdi realized that in the dramatic frenzy of a climactic scene, you need something to burst through the din and be heard. So he invented the concept of *la parola scenica*, "the scenic word," where one word can command the stage and the audience's attention. This is when the soprano interrupts a raging orchestra to cry out, "Peace!" Or Rigoletto's unforgettable phrase "I want my daughter!" When the tenor backed by a chorus cries, "To arms!" or "Long live freedom!" or "Save our homeland!" you know it's time to fasten your seat belt. These are words that even if you're not following what the hell is going on, or you don't speak the language, are immediately arresting. The rest of the music and the scene mean much more when la parola scenica is invoked.

It occurred to me that I had seen this before. Small architectural gestures can also influence your understanding of a scene as it appears in your life. And this is what I have come to consider architecture in the service of meaning. Meaning comes from how people relate to their space. How does it make them feel when they walk in the front door? Do they feel they are living a charmed life on a brownstone block in Brooklyn, as if in a romantic comedy at the movies? Do they want their space to calm them down after a hard day of work? Does it evoke the past, nature, safety? All apartments must meet the basic needs of life—heat, shelter, clean water. But the interesting part is how real estate development lets you take bricks and mortar, landscaping, wood, glass, location, numbers, zoning, capital, and heart and create something meaningful.

My first job after college was in Eleven Madison Avenue, a limestone and marble temple of American business that was designed in the 1920s to be the tallest building in the world. I walked into the lobby in June 1997. I had been hired into the Mergers & Acquisitions Group at Credit Suisse First Boston. Everything was white marble. The ceilings soared. Allegories depicting the triumph of American ingenuity were carved into the walls. Industry. Thrift. Patience. Labor.

It felt important to be walking into such a beautiful and imposing place (we hardly ever left). Whether the tasks of the day were major business decisions or mundane minutiae (as was often the case for a first-year analyst), you felt the prestige and significance that emanated from those marble walls. I had very little idea what mergers and acquisitions were or what I was doing, but I sure as hell was going to find out!

The architects who designed Eleven Madison in the Roaring Twenties for New York Life Insurance Company wanted their skyscraper to convey stability and power. It was to be a symbol of the company that commissioned their work. The Chrysler Building, the General Motors Building, the Woolworth Building—all were designed to represent great American companies.

The 1920s saw a gripping contest between several companies to build the world's tallest skyscraper, unleashed by the recent invention of structural steel and the elevator. In the case of Eleven Madison, that dream was never realized. When the building reached the twenty-ninth floor in 1933, at the height of the Great Depression, work stopped, never to resume. The resulting bulky building, with thirty elevators designed for the original hundred-story height, became another powerful symbol—a warning against the excesses of boom times.

Around the corner from Eleven Madison was another parable for how people create meaning through architecture. Mr. E's first office had been in the neighborhood. I remember my grandfather telling me, in front of the courthouse just across Madison Square Park, the New York Appellate Division Courthouse, how happy and proud he was to be an American. Carved in marble on the exterior are famous jurists and lawgivers of history—Solon, Confucius, King Arthur, and others. Only a great country would care to make a place of justice so beautiful, he mused. Having grown up in a place where justice was not always served, and equality under the law was not offered to his people, this building symbolized America's justice system and moral uprightness. Coming from a country where Jews were humiliated and shunned as ritually impure, he was particularly touched that one of the statues would depict the Jewish prophet Moses!

I came to realize that beauty and architecture weren't extravagances, excess costs to be avoided like the plague, but vessels of meaning that could make a real impact on the bottom line. They were in a sense the physical manifestation of your business plan to your customer. And maybe a small gesture could go a long way.

Meaning

The room was simple: a wooden cross hanging above a cot with starched white sheets. No other adornment was to be found on the white walls, aside from a window that looked out on fresh white laundry drying on a clothesline amidst the trees. I had one roommate who also had a small bed. I was staying at Domus Pacis in Rome, a Catholic monastic retreat situated among pine trees for pilgrims to the Vatican. It was a long way from New York City.

I had just left my finance job at Eleven Madison to seek adventure and find my calling, and I had found my way to Rome to participate in a semi-professional performance of *Il Barbiere di Siviglia*. I had the opportunity to practice Italian and study the opera, culminating with a performance in the title role of Figaro in the courtyard of Sant'Ivo alla Sapienza. Our troupe was stationed at Domus Pacis, where all rehearsals, meals, and accommodations were planned for several weeks.

During these weeks we worked doggedly to master the opera, particularly the comic recited banter with harpsichord accompaniment called *recitativo*. Nailing the comic timing in another language was no easy task! Fortunately, Rossini had set the music with such genius that you just had to approach it with the right spirit to capture the humor. The story goes that when Rossini went to meet a deaf and ailing Beethoven in his attic apartment, Beethoven greeted him warmly as the composer of *The Barber of Seville*, while cautioning him against working on more serious music contrary to his mirthful nature.

After a few hours of intense rehearsal, we would adjourn to the Domus Pacis dining hall. As if on cue, enormous bowls of steaming hot pasta would emerge from the kitchen. We would gorge ourselves on penne, gnocchi, whatever the pasta of the day happened to be, and a glass of water or wine. The pasta was incredible. For the sake of the comedy, I had to hope they didn't serve the gnocchi, or I'd be hard pressed to complete the afternoon and evening rehearsals with the ebullience dictated by Rossini!

Come nighttime, that room with the tiny mattress and a view of laundry drying between the leaves felt better than any Four Seasons. I'd take the sense of camaraderie around that steaming hot pasta over any gourmet cuisine. What was for all intents and purposes a monastery, designed for religious reflection in an ambiance of humility, made for the perfect home to pursue music with passion. It struck me how when one is engaged in meaningful work, in this case a comic opera, you don't need a palace. This realization would have a significant impact on how I design apartments.

Years later, I had a flashback to Domus Pacis in a course on marketing at Harvard Business School. I was struggling to figure out exactly where I belonged in the world of business, since I really disliked consumerism and didn't find a lot of joy in material goods. I was reading a case study on IKEA, the Swedish furniture giant, and its founder's belief in a principle he called "Low Price with Meaning." He believed in delivering a low-cost product to the consumer, but not one that was merely cheap. So he infused his furniture with Scandinavian design, a modernist school of natural woods and simple white surfaces.

Scandinavian minimalism calls for the most simple and modest forms in lieu of ornamentation. It can be beautiful, with its clean lines in blonde birch or oak. IKEA turned modesty into a virtue through design. A skeptic would say that they jammed cheap goods on the consumer. To add insult to injury, you had to assemble the pieces on your own! Another way of looking at it is that by making kits to assemble at home, IKEA allowed people to take part in creating their own furniture. They could save money and also engage in a little physical artisanship, which is rare in a white-collar society. This do-it-yourself ethos also contributed to Low Price with Meaning.

I recently read a news article about a couple who fell in love when he helped her assemble her IKEA furniture. They went in for Low Price with Meaning and came out with more than they bargained for!

As we examined other cases in the class, it became apparent that many admired companies espouse a spirit of Low Price with Meaning. JetBlue, for example, is a low-cost airline that decided to make the experience of flying more fun and put a television in front of every seat. You might not get a three-course meal on every flight, perhaps there was less service, but you'd get a happy vibe, catchy advertising ("Without you we'd just be a bunch of TVs flying around"), joyful fonts and logo, and a good TV. Most importantly, it got you from point A to point B at a lower price with a smile.

Domus Pacis existed everywhere. All you really need are the essentials, including a secure place to lay your head to sleep. But you need the basics with meaning. Otherwise, they may be perceived as a deprivation. Many travelers would see the meager room with the tiny bed and the cross as lacking in luxury and comfort. I found it just right to experience the joy and meaning in opera. Good things can come in small packages.

Inspired by Domus Pacis and Low Price with Meaning, it hit me that perhaps we could make smaller apartments where people could pursue their passions in a great city at an affordable price. This strategy turned out to be a fantastic success, but initially people were highly skeptical that a small unit could deliver the goods.

There was one line of units in The Bond that was the toughest sell. It was a large one bedroom, and a lot of the windows looked directly at a neighboring building. It was not entirely a brick wall, but it was not exactly Central Park views, to put it mildly. I decided to make it the "economy two bedroom" and carved out another bedroom so two people could share. I also had our carpenters construct an inexpensive built-in bookshelf with sexy recessed lighting above to call it out. I figured if you don't have great views, why not make something special for people to *oooh* and *aaah* over. I got a lot of ribbing for this one. One newspaper compared our project, sight unseen, to living in a "matchbox"!

It turned out that the economy two bedrooms went like hotcakes. People appreciated a slightly cheaper option to share. And to this day, everyone who rents in that line of apartments loves the built-in bookshelves!

We came up with a host of little details that we thought would bring people a little happiness like the bookshelves. We used wider than usual Venetian blinds and floorboards, because a slight variation from what people were used to made it fun and fresh. We were the first multifamily building in North America to have Nest self-learning thermostats in every unit. The beautiful design and wireless functionality let us greet people with an element of surprise, and it was good for the environment. We even decided to change the door numbers from the conventional uninspired style. We used large letters instead of numbers, and finished them in polished chrome in a beautiful unconventional font designed by the German graphic designer who had created the font used by *The Economist*!

People loved that someone had been thoughtful in designing their space. It gave them a little boost in a town where those don't come cheap. This experience revolutionized my idea of what apartment design is all about. People didn't need more of the conventional wisdom and generic apartments. They needed the essentials plus delight. Ultimately, people animate their spaces with their minds, with their loves, their friendships, and their own bowls of pasta. As developers, we can aspire to satisfy people's essential needs at a reasonable cost, while delighting them as well.

I've definitely enjoyed making luxurious accommodations for those who can afford them, where money is no object. That's a lot of fun and you can really splurge. But I find the greater and more exciting challenge is to create meaningful spaces that people can afford with the spirit of Domus Pacis. Maybe IKEA was on target about something fundamental to human nature. I was ready to learn—ideally with a hot bowl of pasta waiting!

Respect

I think I was channeling my grandfather when I brought a bag of clementines to meet with the remaining tenants at The Alden. All four of them. They had survived a slumlord experience like none other. Eviction by natural and man-made disaster. The building had been the site of a murder years earlier. The landlord had let the elements devastate the place to get the low-income tenants out so the building could be redeveloped. He wanted the building vacant because in 1980 the District of Columbia had passed a law giving tenants the right to form associations to buy and redevelop their building with the assistance of a developer.

The Alden was the first apartment building I kind of fell in love with. Love at first sight is not the best way to buy a building! But we also did our analysis and saw the potential for a major renovation. It was an architectural beauty, built in 1904 as one of the first apartment houses in the United States. The Alden was situated on one of the highest points in the city, on one of the most picturesque corners in DC, surrounded by a nineteenth-century stone church, exquisite gardens, and beautiful historic details in every direction.

At the dawn of apartment living, no one knew quite how to make an apartment building work. This architect had looked to the town house as a prototype, creating a forty-four-unit building out of what were essentially three supersized townhomes stretched every which way to fit in multiple units. The exquisite but decaying architectural detail evoked the decadence of a lost era, a language I understood immediately from growing up on the West Side. Restoring this building was a challenge that engaged my love of archaeology and echoed my grandfather Mr. E's antiquarian instincts.

Water was pouring in through the roof. The building had been hit by mold, fire, water, drugs, vermin—basically the ten plagues of real estate. A drug dealer had commandeered one of the three inter- connected buildings as his lair. It had been raided weeks earlier by federal agents who had found semiautomatic weapons. I didn't tell that to my uncles who were advising me on the acquisition, or they would have thought I surely had lost my mind! I think I met the drug dealer the day I went to visit the property. He was hanging out and spitting off the back fire escape. The brokers had demanded that I sing a few bars of opera to prove that I was really an opera singer. I'm not sure if the drug dealer liked it, but he didn't ask for an encore.

I sat down with the four tenants in one of their apartments, including the mother of the alleged drug dealer. There was no fur- niture, so we sat on the floor and talked it out. A representative from the Latino Economic Development Company was there to represent the tenants and translate if needed. I was comfortable switching back and forth from English to Spanish directly. I shared the clementines that I had brought, and some cookies. I thought that if I was entering someone's home, I should bring something out of respect. I sat down on the floor with them and listened to their concerns. They had been trapped in a building that was slowly being demolished by intentional neglect. The living conditions were horrific. I think they were surprised that I listened and treated them with respect. No one on the landlord side of the business had ever shown the slightest concern.

I'll never forget a follow-up meeting with one of the tenants. I was sitting on the couch and he was sitting to the side of me in his chair facing an enormous television. I was a little ill at ease in the building at the time because no one knew when the drug dealer might come knocking. The phone rang. I looked over at the caller

REAL ESTATE, A LOVE STORY

ID, and it said "JAIL." This was definitely a cultural experience out-side my comfort zone! But I really put my all into finding a solution that would work for the tenants and gave them my full attention.

I still lost the deal. The contract purchaser had agreed to match our offer and had a capital partner out of Chicago. The tenants and their advocates felt comfortable they would close. I put this down as a great learning experience that was perhaps not meant to be.

Six months later, I got a call from the broker asking how quickly I could close. I had lost the original deal, but I had one more shot to do it if I could act quickly. The other developer's Chicago capital partner had backed out. I think they realized that in the months that had gone by, the condition of the building had deteriorated beyond repair. In my idealism and love of the location and the historic building, I wasn't as concerned about the insides. I was planning to redo those anyway. But not quite on the scale that we had to once we opened up the walls and saw the true condition of the building!

Because we had respected the tenants, and shared oranges and cookies on the floor of their burned-out, collapsing building, they were already comfortable with us. They wanted to take us up on our offer. We said yes and went to work.

Restoration

The historic restoration of that 1904 masterpiece was a labor of love. It really marshaled forth some of my favorite parts of the real estate business—architectural history, loving craftsmanship, and doing right by people. The building had tons of architectural details that needed repair, and we were working under the supervision of the DC Historic Preservation Office. We worked with an architectural historian to understand how the building had been constructed and what elements were original. It had bay windows and a beautiful slate roof, as well as a rotted-out entrance. One of the tenants put his foot through the staircase and almost landed in the basement.

The building had hardly been touched in a hundred years. Every mortar joint had to be raked and then mortared anew, and an E-shaped courtyard building has an awful lot of bricks! I learned that the pH of the new mortar had to match the original, otherwise it would slowly eat away at the masonry. So we used nineteenth-century lime-based mortar. It was almost like opera, with its historic costumes and instruments, but for a building. We probably mixed the mortar a half dozen times before we got the right color and pH.

Then suddenly everything went wrong. When I set out to renovate The Alden, I thought I was going to do everything myself, like some kind of Byronic hero on the battlefield with bullets whizzing by in every direction. I thought I could stand at the center of the renovation of a deteriorated historic building and command the troops without the help of an architect, engineer, or large-scale contractor. I had heard tales from my uncles of how they did it in the old days, but things seemed to have gotten a lot more complicated since then!

By sheer willpower we managed to muscle through the bulk of the development. But just when the kitchens started to arrive and we were ready to put the finishing touches in, water began to appear on the floor of the nearly finished basement. We couldn't figure out where that water came from. To be absolutely sure the basement was waterproof, we had to dig up the slab, redo all the sewer lines, lay gravel, pour a new concrete floor, and coat it in epoxy. Basically, we had to start from square one while the rest of the building was held in suspended animation. It was pretty painful, but I learned my limitations. Thank goodness we had bought with a margin of safety, otherwise it might have been a different story!

When the building was finished, we welcomed tenants from around the world and the District of Columbia to live there. We kept our word that the previous tenants would have the right to return to the newly completed building. They had survived decades of slumlords and now had a brand-new place to live. It was a moving experience for me, the ability to use history and arcane knowledge to physically restore an architectural masterpiece that had played a small role in the history of the American city.

Restoring The Alden required hard work and consummate artisanship. But the redemption of a slumlord-decayed, drug dealer–dominated property was possible. And so was respecting the tenants who had never been shown respect before. It was a kind of humanistic vision for the profession that really lit a spark in me. One of the joys of business is mixing with all kinds of people. While I want to make money in business and build wealth, I don't want to get rich and sequestered. My grandfather's oranges had pointed the way to a meaningful and profitable career in real estate.

Purpose

My farewell to opera, or so I thought, was dying on stage in *The Love of Three Kings*. I put all my passion into that tragic death scene, where I played a young king who died for his love. It was a symbolic death and a new beginning for me. With that climactic performance, I handed back the torch of meaning to the world of opera. I was ready to start at Harvard Business School, which promised to be another kind of transformative experience.

I was back in Boston, but I was sure that things would be different this time. No more lonely nights at the library trying to master all of social science in one sitting; I was going to go out for beers with the best of them. I got an apartment in Cambridge near Harvard Square so I would be in familiar haunts and so I would have a little taste of beauty crossing the Charles River every day on the way to class. It was a beautiful experience seeing the river in all seasons—except during the winter, when arctic winds seemed to have a particular fondness for that path!

At Harvard Business School I tried to figure out what to do with my life in business. I was troubled because I didn't feel a calling like other people. Was I an entrepreneur? Maybe a diplomat or a professor? I didn't like risk, yet I loved adventure. I wasn't sure if I was cut out to do business at all. Like the real-life legends of my family, I wanted to do something meaningful, something independent and profitable, something inspiring and creative, and something that would help others.

During orientation we were split into teams and had to complete a treasure hunt. To my surprise, my team nominated me to be the leader of our group. After the hunt, one of my classmates, Avi, took me aside and told me he thought I had the potential to be a leader. This was something new to me. My path had always been a solitary one.

The mission of Harvard Business School is to educate leaders who make a difference in the world. But I wasn't sure what leadership was, or even if I had any interest in it. I was comfortable being a performer and an individual, but unsure about leadership.

I remember one very exciting moment in my section, a group of ninety classmates from thirty-three countries who spent our entire first year learning together. HBS uses the case method, where every class is a simulated real-life situation. You have to chart your own course of action given the facts at hand. It is an interactive method and there are no lectures. There was a finance class on a British land company, and we had to figure out how to strategically sort it out. Somehow, I was selected as the CEO, and I had to grill and cajole the class into giving me recommendations. It was kind of like being the conductor of the orchestra, and I liked the feeling.

Several months went by, and Avi and I became friends. He suddenly felt strange muscle spasms that awakened him in the night. Avi went for some medical tests and they diagnosed him with ALS, Lou Gehrig's disease. They gave him two or three years to live, tops. A few weeks before, he had been living his dream of studying at Harvard in between visits from his girlfriend. Then he received a death sentence.

One of the more incredible things that occurred while I was at HBS was that Avi overcame this life challenge. I think I would have turned inward and despaired. Instead, he resolved to find a cure for ALS, and over several years organized an innovative and entrepreneurial nonprofit to catalyze a scientific breakthrough. His efforts met with success. Avi was able to finish HBS a year later. He has lived the last fifteen years as if they were his last. He has made a profound impact on those around him and on ALS research.

Avi wanted to do a prayer session and bring everyone together in the HBS chapel. He asked me to sing and lead a prayer in song. I sang "Pietà, Signore," an Italian baroque prayer asking God for mercy. I did a small part to bring together a community that was grappling with the shock and pain of learning what was happening to our friend.

It was one of the most powerful moments for me at HBS. I was trying to hide my musical side, my spiritual side, and become a businessman. I wanted to give it my all, just as I had done in opera. So I reconnected with my business past—my financial experiences at CSFB and in real estate—and divorced myself from opera. It was too painful and too confusing to play with my own emotions like that. But for a brief moment in that chapel I was uniting the various aspects of my life in one room and in one person.

In my second year, I took the Real Property class with Arthur Segel. Arthur is a terrific human being who gives of himself and had worked in the public sector before creating a major company. I loved the class. Professor Segel became a great friend and an inspiration, showing that one can combine passion for teaching and mentoring with a very successful business career, entrepreneurship, and giving back to humanity.

Professor Segel also introduced me to his friends that he thought I should work for. One of these was Sam Plimpton at The Baupost Group in Boston. The firm had been started by Seth Klarman when he graduated from HBS in 1982, and it felt like a very small community engaged in an intellectually rigorous enterprise. It was all very exciting. I met the team and underwent those twenty hours of rigorous vetting that I have recounted above. In the end I was offered an analyst position. It felt like a tremendous privilege.

Temptation

I turned down the offer to work in Boston for Baupost, even after the truly transformational twenty hours of interviewing, because I honestly felt afraid I'd be lonely there. I loved New York. It was my home. I hadn't met anyone I wanted to make a life with while at HBS, and I thought I'd have a better chance in the Big Apple. It was a tough decision, and I was pretty sure I had made a big mistake. Something told me that a place built on sheer intellect would be very compelling, and the brotherhood of value investors really seemed like my place. But my inability to create a whole life in Boston would leave things incomplete. To this day, I wish I had the chance to do that fascinating job!

I moved back to New York and got to work as the first hire in a new platform called Square Mile Capital that would focus on special situations, distressed debt, and mezzanine lending. The founder, Jeff Citrin, built a successful business under the firm Cerberus called Blackacre (the fictional estate that is used as an example in real estate law). I joined for the prospect of working with astute investors and being part of the creation of a new company, and for the chance to start a life back in New York. There were two other employees when I started, a brilliant young Wharton grad named Anoop Davé and a talented intern who was finishing his JD/MBA at NYU, Jared Kushner.

When we first started, I got to work on lots of quirky, interesting deals. Jeff's unique vision was to use deductive logic to figure out deals. He could infer from context and the fact pattern whether a deal was likely to be good or bad. Just the story line of why the deal sponsor was looking for capital would give clues as to the merits of the deal. The problem was that this system required trusting that the other players were acting rationally, and assuming they deeply understood the real estate.

While I didn't understand sufficiently what was going on macroeconomically in 2006 and 2007, I was uncomfortable with high prices and stuck to my instincts. I soon became known as a kind of Dr. No in the office, a place where potentially exciting deals went to die. I said no to turning swampland into equestrian estates in central Florida. I questioned whether a judge would rule with the landlord to void New York State law and decontrol a large low-income housing complex that had been built in the 1930s as what was called a limited equity project, meaning that your return on equity was statutorily limited to 6 percent on what had been spent—in 1930s dollars! That meant that this 1,590-unit complex was legally only allowed to earn a few hundred thousand dollars a year. My experience in the New York housing market suggested that judges were unlikely to be very sympathetic in this situation.

I said no to refinancing a huge land development play in Las Vegas. After flying around in helicopters and hearing the mantra "They aren't making any more land in Vegas," I concluded that there was sufficient land, thank you very much. But I was torn between trying to be a really good employee and sticking with my investment principles. Members of the firm seemed really excited to be doing these deals that I spiked.

I was a pretty dedicated employee. During a trip to the rain forests of Central America, I was working hard on trying to see if there was any way I could accommodate the Las Vegas deal in any format. The company was burning through cash and increasingly desperate for a cash infusion. I had to get on a conference call but realized there was no cell phone service. I was told that if I paddled a kayak a good bit out into the water, I could do a quick conference call. I paddled for a half hour with poisonous jellyfish on all sides, and I did the call around noontime. When I came back, I realized that I had been out there for hours, and my reward was an epic sunburn!

After awhile it began to seem like deals that needed to get done didn't involve me for fear that they'd get derailed. That's when I began to wonder if this was the place for me. The way the company was investing wasn't in line with my worldview and risk-averse investment principles. I felt sidelined as a result of that. I wanted to get into the fray, but the deals were too expensive. It wasn't until I began to see the complex and intriguing deals of the subsequent downturn that I realized I had to find the courage to set out on my own. Before I left, I did get to do one fascinating deal that showed the potential of complex value investment, while also helping me discover the power of real estate to transform a neighborhood.

Transformation

There is one place in New York that is more depressing than all others. For me, that place is the unmarked drop-off of the Prison Bus. There is no plaque or canopy or light or joy there. Just a long line of women, eyes cast downward, children in tow, going upstate to visit their men in prison. As a child, I remember seeing their sad eyes in Columbus Circle, walking home late at night not far from where I grew up. As New York changed, Columbus Circle welcomed the Time Warner Center, and the old statues were re-gilded. The Prison Bus moved to Long Island City.

That was where I was sent to scout out a new deal at my new job at Square Mile after business school. Long Island City was just beginning to show signs of life. Parts of the waterfront by the Pepsi Cola sign had sprouted a few apartment buildings, but that was it. It seemed like no place in New York was immune to the forces of rebirth and renovation. But if there was one place, this might be it!

The property I went to look at was a hulking municipal garage in Queens Plaza, where in the early twentieth century a ghastly extension of the Queensboro Bridge had torn a vehicular hole in the neighborhood. The shrieking twist of an elevated rail car greeted me as I approached the five-acre garage of bare concrete, a brutalist brainchild of 1970s urban renewal. Queens Plaza had become an urban planner's nightmare. And the Prison Bus was just a couple of blocks away.

At the same time, the site had potential. It sat atop several subway lines. It was just five minutes by subway from midtown Manhattan. The Bloomberg administration had rezoned the area for high-rise construction, hoping to lure companies to this transit-rich location. The municipal garage site alone could host millions of feet of development and thousands of residents or employees.

The land was owned by the City of New York and leased to a family that owned a sporting goods company with some fifteen years remaining on the lease. Tishman Speyer, one of New York's top office developers, had approached the sporting goods family and the city with an audacious proposal. They would spend the time and money to design a beautiful office tower and secure an anchor tenant for a building on part of the site, in exchange for a long-term purchase option on the entire site. This would take several years and a lot of effort. At the time, people weren't exactly lining up to move their office headquarters to Long Island City. The sporting goods family took the deal, and Tishman got to work.

After several years searching high and low for a tenant, the Bloomberg administration came to the rescue. They wanted that five-acre municipal garage torn down so the neighborhood could come back to life. And they were willing to sign a twenty-year lease for half of the building. A new home for the Department of Health would anchor the transformation of the neighborhood with thousands of new employees. With a New York City AA-rated lease, Tishman could go to lenders and investors and get capital to build the building. But the city wanted the developer to build the rest of the 600,000-square-foot tower on spec, meaning without a tenant in mind. That way the city could leverage its investment to attract private industry.

One day we got a call from the attorney for the sporting goods family, Rob Ivanhoe. His client had an interesting conundrum. When they signed the contract to sell the land to Tishman years earlier, they had inserted a clever twist. They retained the option to invest 50 percent of the equity in the project. This option on an option was in a sense an insurance policy—against feeling like a fool for having sold early if values went through the roof! With the lead tenant in place, this was quite a valuable option. But now, if they wanted to participate, they were being asked to put up $90 million within a matter of months!

We considered making an investment in this new office tower alongside the sporting goods family. On the plus side, there was one major office building in the area, housing Citibank back office employees. On the minus side, that solitary tower had been built in 1990! Since then, no one else had dared. Long Island City had always been up and coming, but never up and came. What was to guarantee that things would be different this cycle? The fate of this unloved corner of the city seemed uncertain at best.

The deal was really complex, but it had a kernel of embedded value. The land acquisition basis was just $25 per square foot, nego-tiated years earlier when no tenant was in sight. That seemed really cheap. The project was partially leased to New York City for twenty years. But there was no control associated with the sporting goods family's option that we could buy into, just a seat to go along for the ride.

My bosses, Jeff and Craig, with their noses for complex situations as a source of value, jumped on it and had me carry the ball with the negotiations. After much back-and-forth, we found a way to craft a joint venture with the sporting goods family. Then we faced another problem. Tishman Speyer had created a great opportunity with the land and the City of New York. They didn't want to give half away! We were in a sense making a claim on the insurance policy they had written. They had their financing lined up and were ready to go. So they sought to make our 50 percent as unappealing as possi-ble so we'd drop out. The construction budget was enormous and included everything but the kitchen sink. It was the first time I was truly confident that a construction job would come in on budget!

After months of further negotiations, the city offered to lease the entire first building for the twenty-year term, with one important caveat. Our side agreed to build another building on the larger site in the future, without a city lease. There was a million-dollar-a-year penalty for not doing so. The city had really stepped up to make sure the project was viable, and we were there to do our part. But Tishman cleverly negotiated the penalty agreement to last twenty years—longer than the life of our investment fund! While this penalty wasn't Tishman's ideal outcome, it did have the silver lining of making it almost impossible for us to exercise the 50 percent option. Somehow, we managed to insert language making the penalty prepayable if we needed to get out early, so we could join the sporting goods family and invest. We signed the deal and prepared to go vertical.

Then the financial world collapsed. Lehman Brothers failed. AIG was rescued by the Federal Reserve. The Secretary of the Treasury approached Congress requesting a $700 billion package to bail out the financial system. There were certainly moments of angst in considering this investment. We wondered if New York City itself could go under due to its dependency on a rapidly disappearing Wall Street for its tax base! But we bit the bullet and went forward with a fully leased building yielding a growing annuity of 8 percent for twenty years.

We closed on the deal in October 2008. It felt dicey at the time, but the deal turned out to be a home run. It was completed on time and under budget by Tishman Speyer. When the economy turned around, it sold for a $100 million profit.

Another amazing outcome came into view years later. Queens Plaza looked very different without the massive garage. The streets were revitalized with thousands of city employees. The municipal garage site was rebranded "Gotham Center." Since then more than a dozen high-rises have sprouted up in the neighborhood, bringing apartments and retail to complement the office development. And Long Island City is no longer depressing. It's now a hot spot.

This was another important lesson. With vision from policy makers and builders, a neighborhood could be brought to life. That opened my eyes to new possibilities in real estate investment and development. While I'd always like to buy cheaply in a neighborhood that is great right now, I am more open to buying in a place that I believe has the right stuff, and the right catalysts, to become great soon. It was a long way from the Prison Bus to Gotham Center. But the journey had shown that transformation is possible on a larger urban scale.

Courage

The courage to begin something new often is born from the ashes of failure. It was an unsettling time in New York City. The credit crisis and financial collapse began to give way to the widespread misery of the recession. I remember watching with excitement as Barack Obama took office. It held a lot of promise for new beginnings.

On Christmas Eve of 2008, I drove to Palm Beach Gardens to look at an investment on behalf of Square Mile. It appeared to be one of the best I had ever seen. A mortgage on a huge, high-end shopping center was being liquidated for a fraction of its face amount. It had a Whole Foods, a movie theater, a Starbucks, and more. The trouble was there was a cotenancy clause in the leases, meaning that if one tenant left, others that depended on it for foot traffic could also leave. The tenants were falling like dominoes, packing up and leaving or attempting to recast their rents at much lower numbers. But it was still a compelling bargain.

I came back from the trip energized and ready to seize this value opportunity. I was disappointed when we deferred to another firm to take the lead. We lost the deal. Shell-shocked by having so many challenging deals at the company, we weren't yet quite ready to have conviction in the good ones.

Banks were collapsing around us. It quickly became clear that property values had reset, and projects with pie-in-the-sky projections were in deep trouble. Anything that was overleveraged could be kissed goodbye, unless there were deep pockets to back it up. During this period, I grappled with seeing failure firsthand. Failure is part of life and part of any business. What's important is how you pick yourself up and start again. What can you learn from your failures, and how can you avoid repeating the same mistake?

As a result of these experiences, and my character and worldview inherited from my grandfather, I always get nervous before a big acquisition. Even after doing twenty or thirty projects that have worked out. I have a sneaking suspicion that my risk aversion might be part of the secret of my success in this business! When we are embarking on a new project, I work extra hard before committing to a deal to make sure I'm not missing anything. I attack the weakest link in my assumptions without mercy to avoid catastrophe.

I found a book of Japanese haiku that helped me think more philosophically about the crazy crisis unfolding around me. One poem became an unofficial mantra for that troubled period.

蔵焼けて 障るものなき 月見哉

My storehouse burnt down,

There is nothing to obstruct

The moon-view.

—Mizuta Masahide, translated by R. H. Blyth

I decided on a new life. Within a matter of weeks, I proposed to my wife and left my job to venture out into the unknown. I wrote a memo to solidify what my principles were and how I planned to act upon them. I wrote that the key would be to focus on illiquidity to find deals that were mispriced.

At that time, the convertible bond market had collapsed. There was a whole class of mutual funds that were invented just to own convertible bonds. When the stock market tanked, the convertible feature was so far out of the money that they became regular junk bonds. The convertible bond mutual funds saw tons of redemptions from their investors who didn't want to own them. The mutual funds were compelled to sell at any price. I saw that illiquidity went hand in hand with value opportunities.

The public markets reacted very quickly to the financial crisis, but the private markets took much longer to react. For a long time, no one wanted to transact. Owners were under water. Lenders didn't want to take a discount, and the system was gummed up. My memo laid out the conditions under which it would be safe and wise to invest in private real estate markets. I don't think I showed it to anyone, for fear that it would seem arrogant that I thought I knew the keys to business.

I realized I needed a business card with a name, otherwise I'd just be some crazy guy with his deeply set principles and passion for value investing. I wrote out a bunch of names on a sheet of paper, including allusions to my family background, various stones or trees (all mainstays of corporate naming!), abstract-sounding intellectual names (apogee, azimuth, atrium), and a few based on opera.

I wound up going with Aria, as it was the simplest and most beautiful sounding to my ear. I chose Aria Investment Group because investing was something that I believed in, and "group" because it made it sound like an important enterprise (i.e., more than just me and my laptop!). My mother, who is a psychologist and is knowledgeable in these matters, thought it was a reflection of my inner ambivalence about leaving the opera world. There may be something to that. I prefer to think that it was an intimation that I could bring my worlds together, and infuse my business activities with the individuality and meaning I had found in opera.

Adventure

Eva and I got married in March of 2010. It was thrilling, and we were surrounded by friends and family who were rooting for us. Eva was radiant with joy, and I was pretty darn excited myself. The rabbi was Albert Gabbai, who had taught me the ancient Sephardic cantillation to read the Torah for my bar mitzvah. He had patiently shown me the ancient blessings and gave me great pride in my heritage. He even accommodated my curiosity about Maimonides's attempt to reconcile Judaism with reason and Greek philosophy in teaching me *The Guide for the Perplexed*. Eva and I had a wedding contract written in my family tradition in Aramaic based on the laws of medieval Castile. Our families held up the wedding canopy, and we drank sacramental wine that had been made by hand (by foot?) by my great-grandfather. It had been mixed with new wines to extend its life at every significant family event, including my birth.

We were on our honeymoon in Bali, in between platters of exotic fruits, when I discreetly stepped out to check email. We were in hot pursuit of a property. The email read as follows:

Dear Josh,

Eva is not going to like this but we found the deal that we have to do.

Best, David

The note came from my good friend David Arditi, whom I had known since childhood. We had been fifth-grade classmates.

David's parents had traveled the world to pursue real estate development, from Paris to Miami to Saint Barth's, and David traveled with them. We became good friends in middle school, culminating in a ski trip on a glacier and some intense European hiking experiences. One memorable hike to the top of a mountain peak gave us a communal hut experience. Twenty people shared a room and ice-cold showers, as well as the satisfying sleep of accomplishment. This was an early taste of Low Price with Meaning. We ate a dish called *käseschnitt* involving a skillet, eggs, cheese, pickles, and bread soaked in wine, which I'm still trying to track down. Over the years, David and I remained friends and met up when we could in Europe or the States. David came back to America to work in the restructuring group at Blackstone after college. Like me, he had to balance his creative side with a passion for business.

We had reconnected in the mid-2000s when I was in business school and David had left his private equity job to build buildings with his father in Miami. David's dad, Maurice, is an amazing person and a true character. At ninety-three, he still comes to the office every day. He was born in Turkey, and after joining his family in France, escaped the Holocaust by hiding out in the basement of a farmhouse. He then went on to serve in the Turkish army, where he was stationed in a Kurdish unit. With his life experiences and his optimistic character, Maurice represents another archetype of a real estate developer. He's an adventurer and a visionary who was often first to discover an emerging neighborhood. He has a zest for life that is contagious. During the downturn, he would emphatically lecture us on the need to have guts and do business even if we were nervous. I think his lectures might have worked!

In 2007, when I was at Square Mile, David and I had chased one of the more unusual deals we had ever seen together. It was a note held by a subsidiary of the French government after the nationalization of the original lender. It was one of the last remaining vestiges of the 1990s savings and loan crisis and real estate crash. The property was encumbered by a foreclosure and a double bankruptcy, one in France and one in the United States. The original developer, who seems to have been a fairly questionable character, had never made a payment on his construction loan—since 1990. When the bank was nationalized by the French government, the lender dropped the ball. The former owner filed suit, claiming that the statute of limitations of six years for foreclosure had expired, and therefore there was no way to collect the $100 million (now $200 million) of debt!

We traveled together to France to pursue this abstruse, illiquid investment. We met with the government entity tasked with liquidating the piece, as well as the bankruptcy judge who, to our good fortune, was based in Antibes in the South of France. We made an offer, but they ultimately cut a deal with a subsequent owner, who seemed to have bought the property in good faith, unaware of the issue. It took a couple more restructurings and recapitalizations before the property got worked out. During our adventures in pursuit of this deal and others, David and I found that we worked well together. David has the ability to get up every day and face the world with optimism. We are both conservative investors who share a love of great locations and hands-on real estate.

Partnership

The honeymoon email set off a chain reaction that would have a strong impact on my career and my life. The deal involved buying a note from two banks secured by a property at 315–321 Ocean Drive in Miami Beach. The borrower had originally bought one 50-footer on the ocean. He had then bought the neighboring 50-footer to create 100 feet of frontage on the ocean using a large loan from two banks, which he had personally guaranteed. The deal was under water and the borrower had left the United States, apparently abandoning the real estate.

As luck would have it, the bank representative that was selling the note had done business with David and his father before. He knew them to be honorable businesspeople who keep their word. They had also repaid his loan, which in real estate—especially in south Florida—is not always a given! They gave us a couple of months of due diligence to study the note in depth, and to see if we could work it out with the borrower who was missing in action.

During our due diligence, we heard from dozens of people that we were fools to invest in Miami, the epicenter of the condo bubble. In land no less! The most illiquid and dangerous kind of real estate investment. There was a backlog of seven years of condo inventory to work through before any new development was needed.

We certainly doubted ourselves and our convictions when we heard from some of the greatest investors in the United States that it was a mistake. The most direct competitor had been seized by its lenders for liquidation. Most of the luxurious properties were a few blocks away. Furthermore, 100 feet of frontage was married to 400 feet of depth. Under the current zoning, our prospective development would be sandwiched between buildings on either side.

We stuck to our guns. We were buying great real estate at a great price without leverage. The property had tremendous scarcity value as the last undeveloped parcel directly on the ocean in South Beach. None of the other beachfront parcels were available for development, either due to historic protections or because they were splintered into hundreds of condominium units. We knew we had something unique at a good price, and we jumped on it.

As we were putting the team together to pursue this project, we joined forces with Tim Gordon. Tim was David's best friend from childhood and a very smart and accomplished guy. They had worked together at Blackstone in the 1990s. David and Tim decided it was time to set out in business at much the same time that I had reached the same conclusion. Together, we found the guts and the capital to buy 321 Ocean.

Tim is hardworking and trustworthy and resourceful. He also comes from a very interesting real estate background. His father is a kind of idiosyncratic genius who over the years has assembled an eclectic portfolio of financial companies, real estate, and stocks. He acquired valuable real estate through the leveraged buyout of a parking company with his brother, the famous real estate broker Edward S. Gordon. He has a terrific sense of humor. Tim and I had known each other for decades and knew we could trust each other. With a strong sense of camaraderie, the three of us set out to do this investment together.

We were in contract to buy the note, but to access the property we ultimately needed to track down the borrower. He was nowhere to be found. The banks were getting nervous, and so we enlisted them to help us find him. He had ostensibly accepted the idea of a deed in lieu of foreclosure, a deal where he would give the property back in exchange for the bank not pursuing his personal guarantee for the shortfall in repayment.

After months of trying in vain, the bank was finally able to make an appointment to meet him in Paris. As we learned, however, a real estate deed must be signed and notarized on US soil. In a foreign country, that meant at the US Embassy! The borrower signed a bunch of papers in Paris, but not all of them. Some were missing. We didn't know if this was an innocent mistake, or a ruse to renege on the deal.

Suddenly, the FDIC stepped in and closed one of the banks. Through hard work and good fortune, we had already locked in the deal by consolidating decision rights with the stronger bank. But it was a close call that could have derailed the whole deal. Finally, the special servicer of one of the banks was able to track down the borrower again, this time in Budapest. They made another appointment at the US Embassy and finally got the documents signed and notarized. With much trepidation and a fair dose of excitement to be making a value investment with our own hands, we closed on Christmas Eve 2010. It was the start of a great partnership.

My original partners have been my family. They were the ones who believed in me and gave me a shot to do business. My uncles Jeff and Don have been incredible mentors in my life and guides to the real estate world. They appreciate my unconventional way of looking at things, and knowing they're there for me has given me a lot of confidence to take the plunge into entrepreneurship. My mom and dad and brothers have also been incredibly supportive at every step, from banking to opera to business.

As I did more projects independently and in partnership with David and Tim, I realized that it was a lot more fun doing business with great partners than living the joys and anguish of real estate deals solo. It's also easier to share the different responsibilities that come with running a business and developing real estate. Over time, we have built a business together. We have one another's back and make sure that we believe in everything we are doing. The partnership flourishes because each of us can bring his own experiences and personality to the table, his own unique approach to business.

Over time, we've also had the privilege of developing partnerships with some of the most savvy investors in the world, who have trusted us to go out there and do business together. In business, and especially in the real estate business, it's often every man for himself. But partnership is something special that's intended to rise above this. The illustrious jurist Benjamin Cardozo distilled the responsibilities of a true partner in his Supreme Court decision in *Salmon v. Meinhard*. He too came from the tradition of ancient Spanish Jewish exiles firmly planted in America.

> A trustee is held to something stricter than the morals of the marketplace. Not honesty alone, but the punctilio of an honor the most sensitive, is then the standard of behavior . . . the level of conduct for fiduciaries [has] been kept at a level higher than that trodden by the crowd.

The relationship between partners is termed fiduciary, which means "based in trust." Over time, legal scholars have distilled the specific responsibilities parties have to one another. There's a Duty of Care and a Duty of Loyalty toward the other party.

In real estate, one is often called upon to act as a fiduciary for others when one is entrusted with their capital. This is a tremendous responsibility. I'd much rather lose my own money than lose money that has been entrusted to me by someone else.

I've been blessed to find great partners, both among family and friends as well as important investors. My family partners taught me what it means to be partners. They've been amazing to work with and learn from. David, Tim, and I have had the privilege of acting as stewards of capital for some amazing people. We have built those relationships on trust and mutual respect as well as Cardozo's wise words.

Surprise

Something else happened at that time that was truly "only in New York." After giving up singing as a career and feeling the power of my tragic death onstage, I tried to deny the part of me that loved opera. I attempted to be all business, and found my entree through the ethos of value investment. I was intellectually engaged and passionate about the puzzle of investing. But something was missing.

I decided to sing a small role with a plucky New York opera company for fun. I had proven to myself that I could be a real estate investor with a heart, so why not indulge in a small performance? So I turned to Duane Printz, who is an incredible impresario. Each year, she puts on one rare verismo opera with Teatro Grattacielo (that's Italian for "skyscraper theater") in New York. Years earlier, I had appeared with Teatro Grattacielo and even won recognition from my hometown paper, the *New York Times*. Verismo is the school of opera that most emphasizes the dramatic power of the words. If *bel canto* is poetry through music, verismo is drama through music.

Duane cast me in the role of a soldier. A simple soldier without a name, who sings of liberty and its potential to alleviate human suffering. I realized that the words were quite meaningful. The soldier bursts into an impromptu prison as the French Revolution is morphing into the Reign of Terror. He tries to free some innocent prisoners but is rebuffed by the authorities.

The jailer suggests perhaps he cares so much about the prisoners because he has a lover among them. He responds that yes, he has the most beautiful, the most beloved, the most pure lover—his country! Liberty is deliverance from eternal suffering. As someone who loves and appreciates my country and what it stands for, I felt I could deliver these lines with passion and conviction. I sang my heart out for my five minutes of patriotism and justice.

A week later, my cell phone rang. It was the Metropolitan Opera. They apologized for reaching me on the fly, but might I be interested in coming in for an audition? The Met apparently had had scouts in the audience that night who had heard me. And they wanted to hear more. I was blown away. I thought I had given up opera for good. I was a sober-minded businessman and a value investor.

Instead, I found myself leading a real estate investment and development firm by day and singing opera at night. I had my first child, my son Raphael, in 2010. The stars were aligned. I would work hard all day, probing for complex, overlooked opportunities. Then I'd go home to play with my son and help put him to bed. I'd hop the subway to the Metropolitan Opera House, swipe my ID, and go backstage to prepare for the performance.

Backstage at an opera house is a lot more industrial than you'd think. There are costume designers at sewing machines, carpenters building or breaking down sets, and electricians to control the lights. I'd put on my costume, put the sword in the scabbard or the dagger in the belt, and listen for my name on the annunciator in each dressing room. I'd warm up, and then step out onto the stage into the lights. I gave it my all. Bows, applause, a quick shower, autographs, greeting friends and fans. And then I'd go home to check emails and work on deals again! And put my son to bed again.

I was on a high. I had started Aria. I had found joy in life, value investment, marriage, and kids. And I was doing business the way I believed it could be done, inspired by the tradition of Mr. E and the legends of value investment.

It's a special pleasure to sing words you really mean. In *The Love of Three Kings* and in this obscure verismo opera, I got to sing my idealism. And it is also a special pleasure in business to be able to say what you mean and to stand up for others. I had yet to experience this in real estate, but soon I would have my chance.

Leadership

When I was at HBS, we took personality tests to understand our leadership style and figure out what type of businesspeople we should be. We answered a bunch of questions that were plugged into a computer. When we received the results, I was in a category representing maximally 5 percent of the class. The vast majority of the business school class represented traditional leaders throughout history: extroverts, business executives, athletes, type A overachievers. My results were a bit of an outlier. They came out more like Gandhi and Martin Luther King Jr. than businesspeople! They emphasized principles and feeling. It was a style that was conducive to quiet moral leadership, reluctant leadership that steps up to right some wrong.

I haven't come to leadership easily. But my experiences working in real estate have given me the confidence to lead by example, guided by my moral compass. Initially, this derived from value investing, where leadership can be manifested in a brainy outsider. It also came from standing up for myself, our company, and what I believe is right.

Confidence also came from being part of a team that could help realize exciting business prospects. So David, Tim, and I built Aria into a strong company that could train and mentor employees, and work with other developers and help them realize their visions.

My father told me a legend, when I was a child, of how Moses became a leader. In the Bible, Moses initially didn't want to lead the Israelites; he asked God to choose his brother, who spoke better. The legend has it that Moses was a curious child and was playing by the fire. He reached out and grasped a piece of charcoal from the fire and put it into his mouth. After that he could not speak well. So he turned inward. He went into the desert. But he couldn't bear the injustice of his people's oppression. So he stepped forward and went out to meet God, who told him to liberate the Jewish people.

When I was working on Wall Street, I got a taste of another leadership style. I was putting in a hundred hours a week, and one boss seemed to take joy in pushing us hard. I spent my first winter in banking outside Antwerp, battered by the cold, damp wind of the North Sea while organizing company documents and labor agreements spanning twenty-six countries. One night after a few beers, he told me that his philosophy was "management by fear." He wanted to terrorize young analysts into submission, chew them up, and spit them out. Then get new young employees. Part of my approach to honor and leadership has been not to treat others as they have treated me. Many would choose another path, but I insist on according people respect and giving them the benefit of the doubt.

How many of my projects have been bought from slumlords who took advantage of the tenants at every turn? There is a kind of leadership in real estate that comes from treating people with respect. Often past leadership has been so terrible that we are welcomed just for being kind! One of our greatest strengths has been keeping our word and gaining the trust of tenants in the buildings we buy.

Now at the helm of a significant business, I have tried to mentor and grow talent in the ways I wished I had found early on. I could not do it without the belief that we are doing the right thing, or without the strength that comes from partners who have my back. Together, we have built a business and tackled dozens of deals, with care and caution and also conviction.

We have raised a discretionary investment fund to give us more agility and flexibility to invest in accordance with our compass—value investment principles married to traditional real estate values. We have found a lot of interesting ways to pursue such projects, or to partner with or finance others to pursue these goals. We have undertaken our own development projects, often with substantial complexity, staying true to the values that got us here. We have mentored other developers to tackle projects that extend our reach beyond what we can achieve ourselves.

With the increased nimbleness and robust team that has come with our fund platform, we have undertaken the transformation of an obsolete 1960s office building outside Washington, DC, into 338 multifamily apartment units. It's right near the DC Metro Green Line, and we are diving in deeply to bring out the best in the asset. It doesn't hurt that we bought the empty building through a foreclosure sale for twenty cents on the dollar. It's generally really tough to find deals like this in an otherwise up market. Now we are using the principles of Low Price with Meaning to bring it back to life without insane expense.

Community

One of the most powerful moments in my life came about through a real estate project and a close collaboration with the community. It was my chance to stand up for someone. To step up and sing what I believe in.

After we renovated The Alden, the community groups that had worked with us understood that we were honest and kept our word. They saw that we treated tenants with respect, regardless of their income or social standing. The Alden tenants had been represented by the Latino Economic Development Company and Eric Rome, fierce advocates of tenant rights. It was they who recommended us to two tenant associations forming nearby.

Around the corner from The Alden, two adjacent buildings had come up for sale at the same time. They were separated by an over-grown parking lot with a knocked-over chain-link fence. The idea was to try to make a deal with the two tenant associations that controlled their destiny through DC statute and combine the sites. On one side was a really run-down turn-of-the-century building with an elegant but crumbling facade. On the other was a really run-down plain building with hardly any windows, shaped like a stick of butter. One was inhabited by a mix of Ethiopian and Eritrean immigrants and elderly African American ladies. The other building was mostly Latino from Central America. Each building had formed a tenant association that was going to work with the tenant attorney and community organizers to find a way to improve their living situation.

I realized that if the buildings could be unified, this would be an unusually large lot, perfect for an apartment building. I had fallen in love with the neighborhood during the development of The Alden. This site shared its historic fabric and community feel.

A large site in such a beautiful neighborhood was hard to come by, and that would give the development scarcity value. The challenge was that to fully realize the potential of the site, you had to go through a PUD, a planned unit development. That would be a multiyear community-driven entitlement process involving numerous meetings with neighborhood groups, the Planning Department, and the Department of Transportation, followed by public hearings before the Advisory Neighborhood Commission and the DC Zoning Commission.

Undaunted, we dove into the development process. We found a really terrific local architectural firm called Cunningham Quill that had an appreciation for the neighborhood. Our idea was to preserve a portion of the more charming turn-of-the-century building and demolish the smaller stick-of-butter building.

We came up with a creative offer to accommodate the forty-nine rent-controlled tenants who lived in the two buildings. Living conditions were pretty miserable. Both buildings were at the end of their useful lives. We decided to offer the tenants two options: return to a redeveloped or rebuilt project at their rent-controlled rent, or receive a substantial cash buyout that they could use to improve their lives in other ways. They were free to choose whichever outcome they preferred.

A substantial number took each option, and everyone chose one of the two. This meant that the development could proceed through the PUD process to get entitlements to build extra density. Using a classic New York dumbbell shape for the building, we devised a way to fit in a lot of floor area while keeping the building under the sixty-foot height limit mandated by DC law. Additional density would be necessary to make it economically feasible to build brand-new homes for many tenants at very low rents.

The moment of truth arrived when we had to close on the buildings without a clear indication of whether the PUD would go through. It was a bit of a leap of faith, but we felt it was important to keep our commitment to the tenants. Most prudent developers without the entitlements locked up would probably have walked away.

It would take well over a year to work our way through the entitlement process, always in suspense. But because a lot of the tenants were counting on us for cash payments that they needed for surgery or to start a business, we went ahead and closed on the deals. We had confidence we were presenting a worthy project. In the event we failed, we had figured out a way to get out without losing our shirts by renovating the buildings rather than rebuilding them. It wouldn't be pretty, but our principal would be preserved. So we held our breath and trusted that our work with forty-nine rent-controlled tenants and the neighborhood would come to fruition.

We met with everyone in the community who would meet with us. Some hated the idea, some loved it. Some wanted more parking, some wanted less. Some wanted more affordable housing, some wanted less. Very few gave us the benefit of the doubt. But we worked like crazy to win over everyone we could. We met with the neighbors, community groups, affordable housing advocates, the green lobby, the "alley lobby" (don't ask!), and everyone else who would listen. We kept track of the neighborhood meetings we held, and in the end, it was over fifty. We put our heart and soul into making this project work. In a neighborhood that is often skeptical of developers, one environmental activist compared the feeling when we testified in public to "a Bernie Sanders rally."

We also worked with a number of local nonprofit organizations to get a better handle on neighborhood priorities. We offered to tackle much-needed community projects, like renovating the community room at a home for disabled residents, and installing computers for after-school programs for at-risk youth. When the boiler broke at the local day care center and classes were suspended due to the cold, our maintenance engineer (whom we had sponsored for HVAC training) came in and fixed it. By the end of the process we were truly immersed in the concerns of the neighborhood. We really felt committed to being part of their success.

The True, the Good, and the Beautiful

One of the residents took me aside after a tenant meeting. Miss Peggy is a lovely African American lady in her eighties. She is legally blind and had lived in her apartment for sixty years. But the building was falling apart, and no one had heard her concerns about the rats, vermin, leaks, and other issues that arose during a lifetime in her apartment. She wanted me to see it, to be sure that we could make something equal to it in the new project that we were planning on the site. You never know quite what to expect in an old building. The apartments I had visited in The Alden had truly seen better days.

Miss Peggy slid the key into the lock and opened the door. Her home was immaculate. She had a beautiful chandelier and stunning furniture under plastic covers. She was blind and had gone out of her way and up and down stairs to entrust me with her future. I got a lump in my throat. I vowed that we would make sure she was okay and make her a beautiful new apartment.

The day of the most critical public hearing arrived. The room was packed, including a videographer for RT Russian Television who lived next door and was trying to extract benefits for himself by tarnishing the project. All eyes were on Peggy when she got up in front of dozens of people from the neighborhood. She told them that if I hadn't come around, she didn't know what she would've done. She'd probably be homeless. That hit me pretty deep in the gut. It was probably the most meaningful moment in my experience in the real estate business.

My first calls were to my grandmother and mother, because I felt the powerful impact of doing the right thing, and it felt incredible. I hadn't realized I could have such an impact on someone's life. Miss Peggy is a very kind person, and we have supported each other throughout the ups and downs of the project. After many more public hearings, we were approved 11–1 by the Advisory Neighborhood Commission and unanimously by the Zoning Commission. After sixty years of no one listening to her, I have the honor and privilege of building Miss Peggy a brand-new home.

In a sense my journey in real estate has been a little like *The Wizard of Oz*. I had to find a brain, and a heart, and courage. And I had to find the wisdom and experience to be able to deploy them all in my business.

Another prism through which to understand this quest for meaning in work was set forth by the great philosophers Aristotle and Plato. In their conception, there are three ideals in human life and behavior—truth, goodness, and beauty. Each one is part of cultivating a full life. I wanted to find a way to put your whole self into your vocation, where creativity, building, and bringing something into the world could each have a place. These would complement the investor worldview that I drank in as a kid from my grandfather. I wanted to have it all, to seek the three ideals of human flourishing.

Value investment is built on one of these three pillars, truth. The importance of truth is not to be underestimated. A search for truth is at the heart of all great intellectual enterprise. But a broader search for meaning leads one to consider other ways of interacting with the world that use the whole self. Good and beauty also call out to be found.

At various times in my life I have tried to utilize pure reason. I have tried to know everything, and stepped back because it wasn't satisfying. Opera and life experience in the real estate business opened my eyes to other compelling ways of engaging with the world. As a whole person, you want to be involved in making people's lives better, being honest, and making places more beautiful. As a craftsman of meaning in real estate development, you can even make places where there were none.

Reconciling these different parts of a life in business—the mind and the heart, the archaeologist and the poet, the vocation of the investor and the entrepreneur—has been a big part of my career. It has been my secret to unlocking the mysteries of the real estate business and carving a meaningful life out of it.

As I write this, I feel I have found a way to bring all the strands of my life into harmony. My curiosity, faith, honor, passion, and hard work have all found their place. I'm exercising the muscles that were only partially used in finance or in opera in new ways. In building The Clifton for Miss Peggy, I was able to make a difference in someone's life and build a beautiful and significant building. It was acquired through a complex process that allowed value investment principles to work and limited risk. And we found the deal by respecting people and doing right by them.

I owe a debt of gratitude to the real estate business. In a sense, my own calling was fragmented like the broken vase of Mr. E's countertop. With his inspiration and my faith in learning and discovery, I have found my voice, and found a way to be a businessman in accordance with my principles. Thanks to my work in real estate, I have been able to restore that vase to a meaningful whole.

PART II

Real Estate Investment and the Handshake Philosophy

My First Deal

The first building I ever bought came through a horse-racing, chain-smoking Israeli broker who loved art, and a Nepali bed-and-breakfast owner. I found a commercial townhome advertised on the internet in the Adams Morgan neighborhood of DC, at various times an interesting melting pot of Ethiopian immigrant, 90s grunge, Latino culture, and its own unique brew. It had seen better days. Adams Morgan was now home to jumbo-slice pizza and nightclubs, but there was a certain bohemian charm to 18th Street, where seedy and fun came together. It was very walkable (and almost impossible to drive). I thought I'd give it a shot.

I did the "back of the envelope" analysis. That's how you run the numbers in real estate—by hand or in your head. You just need the essentials that you could write on the back of an envelope. Add up the rents from the Pakistani pizza guys in the basement, the Colombian *botánica santería* store above, and the four apartments that would be great for young people with a tolerance for nightlife (there wasn't really a word for millennials yet), subtract out the expenses, and you've got a pretty good cash return. That was before I learned about the flooding issue. We had to send a camera scope down the drain and ultimately extracted several large rags from the grease trap that were clogging the sewer line. Not, however, before several weekends were spent dealing with plumbing emergencies.

Here was a typical conversation with the broker on the deal, Yigal:

Yigal: You'll never guess who I heard on the radio. I'm in the car listening to the Metropolitan Opera broadcast, and you'll never believe it; there's a guy whose name is exactly the same as yours!

Me, in costume: That's funny, Yigal, because I happen to be at the Metropolitan Opera right now.

Yigal: Have you heard of this guy?

Me: Yes, as a matter of fact, it's me.

Yigal: That's not possible, you are a funny guy. You can't fool me. What a coincidence someone else would have the exact same name!

If it sounds like chaos dealing with all these characters, it was. But it was a pretty darn fun way to be an investor.

When I showed up for the closing, it turned out that there was a title issue that I hadn't been made aware of. Evidently, the former owner had a lawsuit against the current one. She had filed a *lis pendens* (lawsuit pending!) against the property, making it virtually impossible to finance. That was why the deal was trading at a manageable price. We found a way to resolve the dispute at the closing table and we closed all cash. As a result of the illiquidity caused by the title issue, the building was bought for a reasonable price.

I was scared to buy my first building in my own company. But I was also excited because I felt I had found something in a really good location for a not crazy price. It showed a good cash return. Once I solved the basic issues, it would have liquidity where there had been none. I remembered my grandfather, Mr. E, telling me about his first day in real estate, when he had found a building he wanted to buy. He had negotiated with the seller and put down a deposit on the property. But suddenly he was struck by fear. With Mr. E's risk-averse mentality, buying his first building was a small exercise in courage.

For me, buying my first property forced me to overcome my fears from the Great Recession. But I felt inspired to be guided by a philosophy that mitigated the risk. The market was down and the world had stopped, but people were still getting jobs in Washington. I spoke to my brother Dan, who lived several blocks away, and we agreed that the neighborhood was an intriguing and compelling place to live. We closed on the deal and got to work.

Real Estate Value Investment

To invest wisely in real estate, you need a method to separate the wheat from the chaff, some way to navigate amidst the blizzard of deals that you see each day. Yogi Berra reminded us that you've got to be very careful if you don't know where you are going—you might not get there.

The conventional wisdom will tell you that value investment is technically impossible in this day and age. The market is so efficient at pricing things that no deviation between market price and intrinsic value is possible. Any bargain will be recognized, trade up, and disappear. This is the efficient market hypothesis that has gained wide currency. I have seen otherwise.

I've been lucky enough to encounter two schools of thought that have proven to be great engines of wealth, while keeping risk to a minimum. They are so good, they're probably one in a million. One is the value investment school of Benjamin Graham and David Dodd, who taught at Columbia in the mid–twentieth century. The other is the fabled school of New York real estate of Mr. E and his peers.

The great value investor Warren Buffett wrote a fascinating article called "The Superinvestors of Graham-and-Doddsville." In it, he traced the investment performance of nine billionaires back to their experiences learning from Graham and Dodd at Columbia. They all ascribed their success to the teachings of value investment that they had imbibed as students. And they all had generated incredible investment returns over a lifetime. Statistically, this should be impossible. But nine outliers from the devotees of an obscure financial philosophy seems more than coincidence.

Value investment is why I turned my life upside down to start Aria in the depths of the Great Recession. In my forty-three years, I have only chosen to start a company once. That was in 2009, a time that the conventional wisdom said the world was coming to an end. The Dow was plummeting several hundred points a day, and banks were failing left and right. It was a frightening time. Everyone I knew was urging caution. But I felt confident that finding great real estate cheaply would mitigate risk. I realized if I didn't take the plunge now, when things were cheap and I could invest wisely, I probably never would.

It's one thing to study and appreciate the philosophy of a couple of bright Columbia professors. It's another to quit a stable job and try to do it in the worst recession in fifty years. Thanks to a recognition that value investment reduced risk, and consequently that the downturn was in fact the best time to get into the fray, I found the courage to go for it. I was able to get into the business while a lot of the big players were still licking their wounds.

I soon realized that another extraordinary business philosophy was hidden right under my nose. It was a treasure trove of investing wisdom and values to live by. It held the mysteries of what makes a neighborhood great, and what makes real estate precious. It was the investment philosophy of traditional New York real estate that I had witnessed in Mr. E. He had a knack for success without taking on a ton of risk. Why did the descendant of a poor girl in Hamadan and her husband in Kashan in Persia, who got married when she was twelve, make it in real estate in New York? This also seemed more than coincidence.

Neither of these great schools of investment provides a detailed blueprint to real estate investing. There is no book that I know of that seeks to apply the principles of value investment to real estate investing. Nor has the traditional, honorable school of Mr. E, the New York real estate School of Hard Knocks, been written down.

This is my attempt to do that. Part of my adventure has been figuring out how to make it work in the New York City of today. After all, I wasn't born in a mud house in Persia, and I didn't attend Columbia in the aftermath of the Great Depression! But I wanted to discover these secrets and put them into action in an authentic way.

The Four Quadrants

Marrying these two schools means seeking great real estate at a great price. The way I see it, value investment helps you find the right price. Traditional real estate helps you identify great property. It's a potent combination. Buying good real estate cheaply gives you a cushion when things go the wrong way, the "margin of safety" prized by the value investor.

My goal is both simple and radical. While it looks obvious, great real estate at a great price is not the goal for most people in the real estate business. Many investors are looking for a specific financial return profile. They use IRR (internal rate of return) as their yardstick to measure a good investment without considering risk. Others want to be in the best location regardless of the price, and will overpay accordingly. Some funds are mandated to buy "safe" cash-flowing office buildings, whatever the price. It's only when the economy turns that people remember that safety is a function of price as well as the asset itself!

I find it helpful to look at it as a matrix, with good and bad real estate on one axis, and good and bad pricing on the other. Four quadrants emerge:

	Good Real Estate	Bad Real Estate
Cheap	**Genius**	**Intriguing**
Expensive	**Hmmmm**	**Oops**

If you're reading this book, you probably know how to avoid the worst quadrant, bad real estate at a bad price. But it's not so apparent at the peak of a bubble, when every swamp looks like a golf resort in disguise!

It's much more seductive to buy great real estate for an expensive price. Look at Stuyvesant Town. A $5 billion purchase turned into $3 billion virtually overnight. The real estate was great—eighty acres in Manhattan. But it was bought for much more than it was worth. When things didn't turn out precisely as planned, the property was seized by its lenders.

Also intriguing is bad real estate cheap. Others have made a lot of money doing this. It is reminiscent of Graham and Dodd's famous analogy between the art of value investing and picking up cigarette butts from the street. There may only be one or two puffs left in those cigarettes, but they're free! During the last downturn, banks had to get rid of all the junk on their balance sheets, and did so at very low prices. More recently, banks have unloaded a lot of undesirable, mediocre parcels in Puerto Rico for pennies on the dollar. Many have succeeded in these types of ventures, and many have failed. You have to be sure you're not buying junk that isn't worth the time and money to fix it!

There is a more stringent standard to which I aspire: to find great real estate at a great price. This quadrant is exceedingly rare. People are not exactly going to give away the best property. So you have to find situations where good real estate is trading cheaply. There's usually a story behind it. There has to be some reason something is undermanaged, unappreciated, unloved, misunderstood, before its time, or broken. Perhaps it's an upside-down capital structure or lack of capital expenditures. Obsolescence. Vacancy. Something people perceive as risky that in fact isn't risky.

If you buy great real estate for a great price, you can weather the inevitable ups and downs. You can tolerate the risk that is pervasive in the real estate business. Who knows what the world will throw at you. But at least if you invest with a margin of safety, you shouldn't lose money if and when things go haywire. I once won a copy of Seth Klarman's book at a charity auction. He inscribed it with these words—half well wishes and half wise admonition—"May all your investments have a margin of safety!"

Focus on Illiquidity

When the Great Recession was still a twinkle in the credit crunch's eye, on September 27, 2007, Bloomberg columnist Mark Gilbert released a telling series of jokes. They were based on "Chuck Norris facts," humorous/serious statements of the action film star's virility and omnipotence. "Chuck Norris counted to infinity. Twice." Or "Chuck Norris can strangle you with a cordless phone." And so on. Gilbert zeroed in on a financial version of Chuck Norris facts that captured the zeitgeist of the credit crunch:

Chuck Norris doesn't supply collateral, only collateral damage. (When many market participants who had borrowed money were being called to supply collateral for their loans)

When the yield on a Chuck Norris bond goes up, the price also rises. (A bond math impossibility)

Chuck Norris trades on fear and greed simultaneously. (Even the legendary Warren Buffett says to be fearful when others are greedy and greedy when others are fearful)

Chuck Norris subprime collateralized debt obligations still trade at 100 percent of face value. (Subprime was taking a bath at the time)

The best of the bunch put liquidity at the heart of the problem:

The tears of Chuck Norris would supply enough liquidity to solve the credit crisis. Too bad he never cries.

When I started Aria in 2009, I wrote a memo expounding my philosophy of real estate investing. Of course, I couldn't get anyone to read it. Then again, I didn't show it to anyone. I didn't know for sure if my ideas would work. Only now am I comfortable sharing them—tested in battle! The memo didn't have a name, because I was embarrassed to even have a memo on investment philosophy at age thirty-three. So the computer automatically named it after the first three words of the document: Focus on Illiquidity. Illiquidity and the special situations that cause it provide the clues to finding value in real estate.

You could do it the other way around. You could look at great real estate and hope it's cheap. I've tried. After a while, my eyes glazed over. In the great wide world of real estate, your chances of finding a cheap price amidst great real estate are slim. But your chances of finding great real estate that slips through the cracks in special situations are higher. Wrestling with distressed deals during the downturn highlighted the value of focusing on illiquidity.

Vista 12 in Miami was a terrific building at a very good price, but it was tied in knots. We knew instinctively it was good, but it took the exhortations of a youthful eighty-year-old to get us to close on the deal.

Vista 12 was a twelve-story building in Little Havana in Miami with a hundred-car garage. Every unit had a balcony. The building had been developed in the subprime era as "affordable condos" with city and county subsidies. When the mortgage market evaporated, construction abruptly came to a halt. Now the bank was trying to figure out what to do with a partially built building. It was billed as 95 percent complete, but 75 percent would have been generous!

We were approached to buy the first mortgage from a regional bank that had bigger fish to fry. The borrower had personally guaranteed the loan, and wanted to hand back the keys in return for getting off the guarantee. But there was a second mortgage recorded on the deed by none other than the City of Miami. This mortgage was not intended to be repaid. It was recorded to ensure the property would remain affordable for twenty years. And it was written for affordable condos, a market that no longer existed! Here was much-needed affordable housing sitting empty.

We felt the building would make a great rental if we could restructure the deed with the City of Miami. It was a brand-new high-rise at a very good basis, around half of what it had cost to build. With a basis so far below construction cost, it was unlikely that we'd face much competition in the near future. It would help an underserved segment of the market, the middle class and working class, that didn't have great housing options.

But it was a catch-22. If we bought the note, and took title through a consensual deed in lieu of foreclosure—where we would get the keys and the past developer would walk without responsibility for the mess—then the City of Miami's second mortgage would take first position. We might still be obligated to sell the building as condos during the housing crisis. Our other alternative was to foreclose. That wipes out any junior mortgages. But we didn't think that foreclosing on the City of Miami would be a good prelude to what we hoped would be a long career in the neighborhood!

We agonized over the decision. We went to speak with David's father. Maurice, in his late eighties, had more vim and vigor than many half his age. He implored us to seize this chance. Good deals at a great price don't stick around forever. Real estate in the best quadrant is hard to find. In Vista 12, a significant price discount compensated for the headaches and complexity. We had a margin of safety, but amidst the tumult and a million details, it was hard to be sure. Maurice's enthusiasm helped us overcome our fears and secure great real estate at a great price.

As soon as we closed on the note, my partners David and Tim sprang into action. They met with a number of stakeholders to recast the City of Miami mortgage so the building could serve its purpose—to provide housing for moderate-income people. It came down to the wire. The Housing and Loan Committee met to vote on the restructuring of the loan. They were suspicious. They thought we were somehow a front for the developer who had blown the project in the first place! In the end, the committee voted to approve the change and permitted the project to move forward as rental apartments.

Getting the final Certificate of Occupancy for a partially built building wasn't easy. It involved dozens of trips to the Department of Buildings over the course of more than a year. Just when we thought we saw a light at the end of the tunnel, we were held up one more time! To get to the finish line we had to rebuild the sidewalk outside the building. But the county controlled one street, and the city the other. They couldn't agree on the radius of the corner! We finally got it done. We got to provide much-needed housing in an underserved community. And we had turned an illiquid headache into a beautiful twelve-story rental building, much cheaper than we ever could have built it.

To find good real estate, you need to know where to look, and you need guts to identify true value when others are running for the hills. Illiquidity provided the map. And thankfully we had the wisdom and youthful enthusiasm of an eighty-year-old to find the courage!

Special Situations: The Brooklyn Bar Menu Generator

Illiquidity is the common denominator between the deals we have just discussed. Chaos, broken structures, and confusion reigned. In each case, we had to get to the bottom of a story. Why wasn't the real estate behaving as it should, and why wasn't the market pricing it fairly? To have conviction in these situations, to go against the herd, you have to think that the market has got it wrong. Otherwise, you are probably the one getting it wrong.

There's a website that I love called the Brooklyn Bar Menu Generator. It's based on the satirical premise that there's an underlying structure to the menu of a hipster foodie restaurant in Brooklyn, to the point that a computer could make one up. When you press a button, an algorithm gives you endless iterations of nonsensical but Brooklyn-sounding menu items like:

Rustic Eggplant Toss with Kale . . . $12

Anchovy with Burnt Sardine Toast & Farm-to-Table Rye . . . $14

Artichoke Frittata with Beer-Braised Lime . . . $9

There's even Salt . . . $10

As I see it, there is a comparable algorithm for finding value investments. Like a Brooklyn bar menu, there is a deeper underlying structure to the principles of value investment. With careful study, these can be equally applicable to real estate investing.

Value investors have some shorthand criteria for finding situations conducive to investment, as in the special situations we have discussed. These are the rare cases where someone is likely to part with something for less than you think it's worth. They look for distressed debt or bankruptcies where someone wants to unload a headache. They look for corporate spin-offs that cut loose a subsidiary. If it's engaged in a different line of business, investors might elect to sell or be obligated to. They look for divestitures or privatizations, where companies or governments sell poorly managed businesses outside their primary focus. It's likely they haven't been managed well, and perhaps there's some upside to reversing that. They look for properties trading below book value. Value investors look for complex structures that most people won't take the time to understand.

In the real estate business, the menu generator would send you special situations with a focus on illiquidity. On the menu you'd find distressed mortgages like Vista 12. The property traded below replacement cost, in a sense the real estate analogue of book value. You'd find land that people once feared or misunderstood, like the drop-off for the Prison Bus in Long Island City. You'd find the fragmented ownership structures of the broken vase variety, as in Bank Street. You'd find divestitures of noncore assets—a company selling a defunct headquarters or a university selling off obsolete dorms. You might also find situations like The Alden or The Clifton, where dealing honorably with individuals and a community is required. The desire to pursue such emotionally committed deals is in short supply!

Value investment in real estate means buying an illiquid, undermanaged, distressed, or poorly marketed property in a great location, and bringing it to its full potential. You start with illiquidity and end with a cash-flowing, institutional-grade, liquid asset. You have to be willing to find value in any form, anywhere on the menu. That is what makes real estate investing so exciting. My partner Tim has distilled this investing ethos into its purest form: we are relentless in finding value but agnostic as to the tools and tactics needed to unlock it.

The bar menu generator of value investment tells you where to look for good deals. But it doesn't tell you what makes great real estate! As we shall see, this is a domain where traditional real estate has the most to offer. Value strategies are complemented by elements specific to the real estate, like location, scarcity, and beauty. If you merely follow value principles deductively to ascertain that it *could* be a great situation but don't use your human faculty for induction, your life experience, and understanding of human nature, you might be making a mistake. Like the bar menu generator, you may be buying a dish that sounds great but tastes terrible!

Location

Traditional real estate is centered on location, and the quest for the next great neighborhood is an obsession for real estate people. In theory, everyone knows what makes a great location. In practice, it's not so straightforward. There's no map of great locations. You have to find what makes a particular hunk of earth useful and meaningful to people.

The worst investment I ever made offered a painful lesson on value investment and the traditional real estate emphasis on location. The Lenox China facility in southern New Jersey was a magnificent red brick corporate campus. It boasted over 400,000 square feet of indoor space with soaring ceiling heights. A large American flag fluttered proudly on the front lawn. The property had tremendous electrical and water capacity due to its history of producing china and silverware for a great American brand.

It also had many of the hallmarks of a value investment. It was a corporate divestiture of a noncore asset. We were getting a great price because it was being delivered vacant. And we were paying a fraction of what it would cost to build a comparable facility today.

Shortly after closing, we were approached by two brothers who owned a large shipbuilding company headquartered nearby. They too had been vying to buy the property. The brothers were known to rise at dawn and do a hundred push-ups in front of their employees. They offered us a million more than we had paid. We thought that filling the vacancy would generate a higher value. That was to be our last great opportunity.

Months went by and no one seemed interested in leasing the property. We spoke to self-storage developers, office users, and tradesmen looking for warehouse space. We even found a canned tuna fish company that liked the tremendous water capacity for their fish processing! But no one took the bait.

The reason for the failure of an ostensibly cheap value investment lies on the traditional real estate side of the ledger. The location was flawed. The facility was close to Atlantic City airport, but that was about it. It wasn't close to public transportation or any major highways. It wasn't close enough to anything to be a great place for people to work. And for many decades, industrial production hasn't exactly been on the rise in the northeastern United States. Production moved to the South, or overseas, or was automated. This was a majestic industrial facility acquired well below replacement cost, with many clues indicative of a value opportunity, in the wrong location. It was a classic value trap.

What makes a great location? Ultimately, it's a function of where people want to live and work, love, reach their professional potential, and find meaning. Location is about human psychology as well as geography. People want to live in great cities where they can get a job. They want to live among interesting and creative people they can spend time with or marry. Often these are found near great universities, which have a long-term or infinite mandate. People also want to feel safe and not get shot on the way to work. Lately, many of these attributes have clustered in the great American cities.

Location can be fickle, and history has a way of changing fortunes. I've seen this most clearly in the dispersal of my extended clan during the twentieth century. At various times, they lived in Morocco, Argentina, France, Spain, Israel, Iran, Venezuela, Switzerland, Austria-Hungary, Poland, Russia, and the United States. Seeing these different choices play out over decades gives you a real perspective on what makes a great location. Argentina went from the bread basket of the Americas to struggling with corruption, dictatorship, and economic instability. Galicia in Eastern Europe went back and forth between Russia and the Austro-Hungarian Empire several times during World War I, with devastating results.

Broad brush, the safest locations to invest in are in a great nation that upholds justice and opportunity. Over the long term, freedom, justice, and the protection of minorities have been more powerful than abundance of natural resources in divining where might be a good place to live and work. In my experience, America is the only country that has consistently aspired to those ideals. Being here is half the battle. But the other half is discovering what makes a great location!

Sacrifice or Blunder!?

A sacrifice in chess is a gambit where you accept a temporary setback in exchange for future benefit. On the surface you appear to give up an important piece. It's really a trap for the other player.

A blunder, in the lexicon of my favorite 1980s Yugoslav chess coach, Mr. Jovanovic, is a foolish error. I got hooked on chess as a kid. I learned a lot from the deep structural thinking encouraged by the game, as well as the Eastern Bloc discipline. I tend to think back to chess metaphors in business, because the game forces you to distill a very complex situation into simple ideas. My best game was when I played the number two kid in the country to a draw. He was also playing fourteen other people simultaneously.

At the moment you make a sacrifice and willingly give something up, it is not immediately apparent if you will ever be compensated. It may well be a blunder. Or, in extreme cases, told with Mr. Jovanovic's gusto, "a catastrophic blunder!" You may be a genius or a fool, and only time will tell.

Vacancy in real estate offers a similar dilemma. On the one hand, vacancy speaks to some of the classic conditions for value investment. With the Lenox China factory, we thought we were sacrificing short-term cash flow in exchange for long-term value. Sometimes this is a good trade and the gambit can pay off well. A property may trade at a discount because it's not at its full potential.

But buying vacancy at a discount is a double-edged sword. You have to ask yourself why the property is vacant in the first place. In many cases, it's vacant for a reason. Maybe it's a lousy location or the building is obsolete. No one needs that particular kind of real estate anymore in that area. Such was the case of the Lenox China facility.

In those cases, buying vacancy can be a catastrophic blunder. Like the value investment bar menu generator, vacancy is only a clue that the deal *might* be cheap. You alone must determine if the value is real. To make value investments in real estate, you have to see if your sacrifice—buying something illiquid, giving up cash flow, buying broken pieces, or the right fact pattern—truly leads to victory. Otherwise it may be a value trap, a catastrophic blunder.

When Clairol decided to move its production out of Stamford, Connecticut, close to one million square feet instantly became vacant. The company's mandate was to make innovative hair products, not to hold real estate. Especially not a big vacant factory that would need a lot of work to retool. So they decided to sell it.

My cousin Greg was negotiating to buy it. Perhaps it would be another Lenox China, a white elephant. As the economy tanked, other buyers faded and Greg was able to negotiate a great price, increasing the chance that it would be a true value investment. He had the guts to close on a million square feet of vacant industrial flex space when the economy was down for the count. For most people, it was hard to imagine the space would once again be useful. It wasn't clear whether it was a gambit or a catastrophic blunder.

It quickly proved to be a shrewd sacrifice. Greg invested in the space and found amazing tenants. NBC Sports wanted a big chunk for offices. But there was a ton of space. No one needed a new factory in the Northeast. Who else could use vast expanses of indoor and outdoor space? He cut a deal with Chelsea Piers to take the rest of the space for a huge sports and entertainment complex. The building was fully leased and flourishing. Checkmate.

Why did this case of vacancy work out where others had failed? It wasn't just cheap—it had the potential to be great real estate. It was price *and* location. The Clairol factory was right off I-95, which carries tons of commuters every day. Great city life and a large

REAL ESTATE, A LOVE STORY

population were a short drive away. The location allowed Cousin Greg to envision a more productive use for the space and attract great tenants using the full ingenuity of real estate development. The price offered the luxury of time to develop the space, and sealed the victory when the property was leased.

Real estate has to be both cheap and good, and value investment strategies work best when married to traditional real estate values like location. That way you can separate the real value investments from the value traps, the gambits from the catastrophic blunders!

Neighborhood

Location is the one thing you can't change about your real estate. So I'd always rather buy a decent building in a great location than a great building in a decent location. At the same time, it's much better to pay very little for what will be a great location tomorrow, than to pay up for a great location today only to risk an erosion of value. So finding a run-down, underutilized building in an up-and-coming location gives you the best of both worlds. This is where value investment and real estate instincts come together.

How do you find a great location? Follow neighborhoods and the people that love them. Cousin Greg, who restored the vacant Clairol factory, is a great practitioner of this quest. On the hunt for a bargain, he was one of the first to advocate investing in the Financial District of Manhattan before that neighborhood made its comeback. He worked with an artist cooperative to do a project in SoHo just as that barren, nineteenth-century warehouse district emerged as a haven for artists, and subsequently a residential and retail hotspot.

I remember Greg talking about Hudson Square before I had any idea what Hudson Square was. It's an area west of SoHo owned mostly by Trinity Church. Queen Anne granted the church 215 acres on the west side of Manhattan in the eighteenth century. It was previously the home of New York's printing presses. It turns out I had actually been there once—to print a prospectus in my investment banking days! Under the stewardship of Trinity Church, Hudson Square has since become a thriving mixed-use neighborhood.

Developers have searched for the mythical next great neighborhood with gusto. Each swears by his or her own formula for finding it. It's a search that tries to decipher the great locations of tomorrow from cultural and economic clues today. Some follow artists. They go where the more adventurous bohemian creative class is moving for cheap digs in fringe locations.

Artists often pioneer the best neighborhoods, searching for spacious but affordable manufacturing buildings with great light to live and work in. They may be willing to overlook some of the challenges to get great real estate at a cheap price. They end up making those places cool and acceptable. In the New York area, SoHo, Chelsea, Red Hook, and Jersey City were all pioneered by artists. I remember once being invited to an outdoor bonfire party on the banks of a polluted canal in the midst of a toxic industrial wasteland. Little did I know that ten years later Gowanus would become a hipster paradise in Brooklyn!

Some developers have followed the gay community in search of the best real estate. Before gay marriage and adoption were as prevalent as they are today, many gay couples might have overlooked a spotty school district or the safety concerns of fringe neighborhoods to live in a beautiful townhome at a good price. They were trendsetters, and straight couples followed.

Others follow great architecture or historic housing stock. Neighborhoods with ornate lofts or beautiful brownstones that have fallen into disuse are the first to be rediscovered. Or one could look to locate next to growing universities. Universities rarely go out of business. They become hubs of culture and innovation that attract knowledge industries around them. New subway lines or public transportation almost always spur growth along their routes for years after they are built.

I've seized incredible opportunities due to location in my career, and also missed huge ones. When I was graduating from business school, I met with the New York Economic Development

Corporation under the Bloomberg administration. They mentioned perhaps I could focus on the renovation of a historic elevated railroad off Tenth Avenue in New York. From a New York perspective, that part of Tenth Avenue was the end of the world. Taxis might go there to be repaired. I thought they were nuts. It turned out to be the High Line, now one of the most visited sites in New York!

On the other side of the coin, I've found good investments in unappreciated locations with great potential. I figured out that the cobblestone, off-the-beaten-path charm of Crosby Street would assume some of the luster of SoHo. I was able to restore a bullet-riddled turn-of-the-century apartment house in Columbia Heights, Washington, DC. David, Tim, and I secured an oceanfront parcel in Surfside, Florida, just before a Four Seasons hotel transformed that laid-back beach town.

Over the years I've learned how to get the feel of a location, expending a lot of shoe leather. Many real estate investors drive by properties. I like to walk, and immerse myself in a neighborhood. I keep my eyes open for hidden gems. I think it's important to imagine what life would be like if you lived there, to meet people and to try to understand what makes a particular neighborhood tick.

I have another secret weapon in finding great neighborhoods— my brothers. They are bright and creative and extremely talented. My brother Dan moved to Washington, DC, after graduate school to work in foreign relations. He lived in a little apartment in Adams Morgan. In DC, I found a lot of things that I also loved about New York. It had beautiful brownstone neighborhoods, public transit, universities, and great jobs even in a recession. It combined historic buildings, civic activism, idiosyncratic laws, and quirky characters.

Getting to know Dan's neighborhood led me to the townhouse with the novice Pakistani pizza maker and the Colombian *botánica* with séances (we ended up with a ramen noodle entrepreneur who had a day job at the NIH!). As Dan moved eastward toward Logan Circle, along with the center of gravity for young energy in the city, we followed with our investments. We always look for good value driven by special situations, but also cases where the neighborhood has a chance to improve around us.

My brother Lexy is a writer and musician who has lived in Harlem and Brooklyn. I take it as a good sign when we are looking at something near him. We ended up redeveloping his old coin laundromat in Brooklyn!

Scarcity

To paraphrase Yogi Berra, irreplaceable assets are really hard to build today. And that is the paradox of specializing in great locations as a value investor. You need to focus on "high barrier to entry" markets where you can't get clobbered by competition. And somehow those barriers have to be high for everyone else but mysteriously surmountable by you. I often wondered why I was knocking myself out to specialize in things that are so difficult. But the laws of supply and demand make scarce assets incredibly desirable.

Great real estate investors jump to buy irreplaceable assets. Sometimes it's a location that can't be replicated. It's on a park or the beach, or close to a timeless university or museum or seat of government. Or it is nestled in a highly restrictive regulatory regime, where zoning restrictions or historic preservation protections prevent anyone from knocking off its success. Irreplaceable assets are so desirable because they can't be inundated with competitive supply. If demand grows over time with economic growth, demand will exceed the limited supply and the price should rise.

This is comparable to the concept of a "moat" that is much beloved of value investors. If a great business with stable cash flows is a castle, the "moat" is its intellectual property (think naming your sugar water Coke) or monopolistic characteristics (think toll road on an important route). These make it hard for others to storm the castle and compete away its outsized profits. In real estate the moat is often location. Location is kind of a small-scale monopoly. So long as property rights are respected, only you can occupy that spot with your building. When we acquired the last oceanfront parcel in South Beach, we took comfort in the fact that the location was irreplaceable.

And scarcity doesn't just benefit irreplaceable assets; it works its subtle magic throughout the real estate business. Consider the corner, the product of rectilinear street grids from New York to Berlin to Beijing. Every block has hundreds of feet of frontage, but only four corners. Each corner benefits from a little bit of scarcity value. The average apartment on a corner gets a little more light than the mid-block building. Sun can come from two directions rather than one. The boss gets the corner office. All else being equal, a corner property grants more access to a scarce resource in the big city—sunlight.

Taking this logic one step further, a corner on a park or over-looking the water is even more scarce. You get the benefits of a corner, plus an enchanting view of nature. Think about how many great properties are located on park-fronting corners, like the Plaza Hotel in New York. Parks are almost never redeveloped, so you have a quasi-permanent right to light and greenery in the city.

But as sure as the sun rises, human ingenuity finds a way around the moat. Scarcity value is hard to preserve. In 2013, a taxi medallion that let you drive a yellow cab in New York City went for upward of $1 million. Huge fortunes were made as taxi cab kings amassed precious medallions. There were only 13,607 allowed to be in circulation, roughly the number that Mayor Fiorello LaGuardia had put in place in 1937. Then came Uber, with a new technology and many more cars on the road. By 2018, the price of a New York taxi medallion had plummeted to less than $200,000.

Scarcity and the value of economic moats were the subject of a recent war of words between Elon Musk and Warren Buffett. The ink had hardly dried on Buffett's annual letter when Musk lobbed over a response—with an attitude. Musk is one of the most talented engineers and entrepreneurs alive today, responsible for creating an immensely popular electric battery–powered car. He is designing a rocket ship company that aims to colonize other planets. Musk's response to Buffett was, "Economic moats are lame, what matters is the pace of innovation."

Not to be outdone, Buffett agreed that Elon had done nice things with cars but wouldn't want to take on the economic moat that Buffett had created in, say, candy. Buffett's company had bought See's Candies many years ago and built it into a large enterprise. See's candies are addictive (I know because my grandmother's sister in California used to bring us their lollipops). Musk responded tongue-in-cheek that he was launching his own candy brand to compete!

Their flippant repartee underscores a much larger debate in business and real estate about how to sustain success in a rapidly changing world. Buffett's approach is to buy things cheaply that he understands, that have barriers to entry, and operate them well. It's worked pretty well for him. Musk worships innovation. He's managed to achieve more than anyone would have thought. Technology and innovation are constantly storming economic moats, scaling high barriers to entry, and changing the way people live. Every industry, real estate included, is the scene of an epic battle between scarcity and disruption. It will be fascinating to see how it plays out.

Even the prized park corner isn't immune to competition. New York developer Gary Barnett found a creative way to make more Central Park frontage. He realized there was no height limit on a certain stretch of 57th Street. Then he spent fifteen years patiently assembling land to build high-rise towers. Projecting dozens of stories over their neighbors, his towers have front-row seats on Central Park—from two blocks away!

One of my favorite pages in the real estate development play-book is to use assemblage and psychology to re-create the value of scarcity—at a lower price. People love living in charming historic districts, but they're almost impossible to develop in. As a result, very few people get to enjoy them. Why not acquire the closest higher-density parcel just outside the regulatory moat and make it fit in? It's a development strategy that echoes Low Price with Meaning.

At my brother's old coin laundromat, we found a sizable site that was a half block outside the exquisite Boerum Hill Historic District in Brooklyn. Brownstones there cost millions of dollars. With thoughtful architectural design and a careful selection of brick, we were able to evoke some of the magic of the townhome blocks just around the corner. We can make these rare neighbor-hoods accessible to more people, and enjoy some of the scarcity value of irreplaceable historic assets. This is one way to overcome the barriers to entry that hold up for everyone else.

While scarcity is an essential attribute of great properties, it's never an excuse to overpay. If your thesis is irreplaceable real estate untethered from value, check to make sure you aren't overpaying. Often you hear phrases like "_____ never goes down" or "they ain't making any more _____." When you hear that, run the other way! They're not making any more eighty-acre sites in Manhattan, but that didn't save the purchasers of Stuyvesant Town, who paid a huge price before the last downturn.

I was once advised that they aren't making any more waterfront, so it's time to buy marinas on a lake in Atlanta. That was before the Army Corps of Engineers closed off the river that fed the lake to save an endangered species. The lake quickly dried up, making it very tough for the boats. Along with a good price, one has to make a judgment call on how good the barriers to entry are, how scarce the asset really is. Otherwise it's a recipe for famous last words.

Honor

In real estate, your word is all you've got. Money comes and goes, but a good name is timeless. The best compliment that one real estate player can give another is that their handshake means something. There are so many risks and complexities and understandings in real estate that if you tried to write them all down, you'd never have time to do anything else. Trust allows players to take action with confidence. A reputation for being honorable and doing what you say you are going to do is vital.

So, what happens when you commit to sell someone a property and they get offered $3 million more a week later? My friend Peter W. is a true New York original. He cut his teeth buying buildings in the Bronx in the 1960s, and maintains a persona part dyed-in-the-wool real estate developer with a little bit of hippie mixed in. After making his money in creative development projects in SoHo and the West Village, Peter now pilots himself around the United States in a propeller plane. He loves the tango. He personally renovates his properties himself, expressing frugality in both costs and in the efficiency of his layouts. He visits his New York projects in a restored antique pickup truck, with commercial plates that allow him to better navigate New York's byzantine parking rules.

Peter had committed to sell me two buildings on Crosby Street in SoHo. It was a time-sensitive deal, and certainty of execution was essential. At the signing table, I realized there were a lot of moving parts and I needed to commit millions of nonrefundable dollars quickly. The gas had been shut down in the buildings and it was the dead of winter, with no way in sight to restore service. Huddled around space heaters in long johns, the tenants seemed ready to revolt. Due to the nature of the transaction, it needed to come off without too much of a hitch. So, pardoning the French, I asked him point-blank to tell me now if he was going to screw me. He gave me his word that he wouldn't, finding it rather quaint that I'd bother to ask, and we shook hands on the purchase contract.

The following week, Peter got an offer for $3 million higher from a Hong Kong investor. That was real money on the table. If he tried to wiggle out of the contract, though, it would cause a real problem for me, and he knew it. But having given his word, he couldn't go back. He acknowledged that he could screw me, but he wouldn't. So he made a proposition. We'd go together and spend three months looking for another property to buy instead of his. If at the end of three months we couldn't find something else, he'd keep his word. Not knowing what he ultimately intended to do, I accepted with great apprehension. Anyone who bothers to tell you they could screw you but won't—instead of just saying nothing—leaves some doubt in your mind!

For three months, we looked high and low for another property to buy instead. Peter found a bunch of deals, but he candidly agreed that all were egregiously overpriced. In the end, Peter kept his word and we closed the transaction. This is the kind of thing that you never forget. It demonstrates the power of keeping your word even if it costs millions of dollars. But there was one last twist to the deal. He insisted that if he was going to go through with it, I had to sing tango at his birthday! And to this day, I have.

Think about the advantage that accrues to the person with a reputation for keeping their word, someone who will follow through on what they say. How many more deals are brought to that person, with the knowledge that a yes is a yes and a no is a no? The real estate business has a lot of people who claim they can do a lot of things. Few back up their words with action.

Treating people with respect, without regard to income or status, is another aspiration of the honorable real estate investor. Most people are polite to people who can do something for them. Fewer people are respectful of those who can't do anything for them. The real estate business puts you in contact with people across the income spectrum. You work with wealthy financiers and impoverished tenants, immigrant workmen and bank executives. Benjamin Franklin observed that you have no choice but to be humble around people above you, and it's courteous to be humble in front of equals, but the mark of nobility is being humble before those less advantaged!

Treating people at all income levels with respect has been one of the best business decisions in my career. We have often been asked to intercede as a "white knight" in cases like The Alden where the tenants have been abused or neglected. Just showing up and treating people with respect has been an amazing and unexpected advantage.

Of course, not everyone has the same idea of honor as you do! I once worked for months with a prospective partner on a series of deals, culminating in a really interesting one on the West Side of Manhattan. When we lost the deal, we drowned our sorrows together. When the deal was revived, suddenly the glory was all his. Heads I win, tails you lose is not the recipe for a great partnership! Choose your partners wisely.

A sense of honor was instilled in me and my brothers from an early age by our father Carlos. It was an ethos that came from medieval Spain by way of northern Morocco, where our family was exiled in 1492. In this culture, keeping one's word is paramount. Principles are not to be compromised, certainly not for financial gain.

One story from my father stands out in my memory. You could almost see the executioner's blade glistening under the hot sun as he held the scimitar high above the Jewish maiden at his feet. She was the most beautiful girl anyone in Morocco had ever seen. Her name was Sol, after the radiant sun. Her neighbors accused her of secretly converting to Islam and then abjuring that faith, a capital offense. The son of the Sultan offered that she could be his bride if she would profess the Law of Muhammad. But she clung proudly to the faith of her fathers and the Law of Moses. The crowd stirred and impatiently awaited the death of an apostate to Islam.

The executioner cut into her throat lightly. Even he couldn't bear to see such a beautiful girl die simply because she refused to submit to Islam. He wanted her to see blood so that she could change her mind and accept Islam to save her life. "Carry out your duty, vile traitor," she cried. With that, the executioner raised aloft his scimitar and beheaded the young Sol.

It was 1834. She was Sol Hachuel of my father's family in Tangier, Morocco. She is revered as a saint by local Moslems and Jews alike.

To be true to yourself and your beliefs, while making your way through a very challenging world, is a goal that my father has passed on to me and my brothers. There are many chances in the real estate business to make a quick buck, but few are those who take the harder path and always seek to do the right thing.

Thrift

Thrift is a disappearing virtue that was central to the traditional real estate mindset, and an area where value investment and traditional real estate come together. Thrift is defined as the quality of using money and other resources carefully and not wastefully. Saving ten cents instead of spending it on a Coke, like Mr. E on the ship coming to America. For self-made individuals of past generations, forgoing consumption often provided the capital to take on entrepreneurial projects. In my father's family in Spanish Morocco, all of the brothers saved up to put my grandfather through pharmacy studies in Madrid. They invested in education. In the case of Mr. E and his brothers, saving money was the beginning of a surplus to invest in real estate.

Thrift and an aversion to waste are also vital in constructing buildings. Just as you can buy a building for less than it's worth, you can also build one for less than it's worth. Peter's aversion to waste led him to carefully manage construction costs and extract value from every inch of real estate. In the case of the Crosby buildings, he had preserved the efficiency of tenement living from an earlier, more frugal generation. He upgraded the interiors and still squeezed three bedrooms into 500 square feet! It was a perfect share for roommates who wanted to live in SoHo and weren't afraid of intimacy.

Love of a good bargain is an important motivator in real estate investing. Thrift is the personal manifestation of a value investment philosophy, one that you feel in your bones. It forces you to invest money slowly and judiciously, with careful deliberation. It reminds you to focus on price to find value, and to eschew the shiny trophy for a cheaper, out-of-favor asset.

Mr. E hated waste and loved to save. He enjoyed squeezing all the juice out of a lemon. As a kid, he showed me how to use every ounce of toothpaste by rolling up the metal tube from the bottom. Any acquisition had to meet a high bar. The joke was that he would ask if any expensive birthday gift was returnable. Similarly, investment itself is a weighty act. You have to make sure you're not (heaven forbid!) overpaying.

One of my favorite articles to read in the news is the story of the frugal soul who has amassed a vast fortune and donates it to a worthy cause. The New Hampshire librarian who worked quietly every day for decades among his books, then shocked everyone by leaving $4 million to his alma mater. The Vermont janitor and gas station attendant who saved every penny, "using safety pins to hold his coat together and cutting his own firewood well into his nineties," according to a 2016 article from CNBC, then donated $8 million to the Brattleboro library and hospital.

Oseola McCarty grew up as a washerwoman in rural Mississippi. She worked every day starting at the age of eight. Every day she would start a fire under her pot, soak, boil, and rinse clothes in the steaming water, and hang them on a clothesline. Then she would iron until eleven o'clock at night. She tried using a washer and dryer in the 1960s, but the results fell short of her standards. Her commitment to saving and giving back was covered in a 2020 *Philanthropy* magazine article:

> She had begun to save almost as soon as she started working at age eight. As the money pooled up in her doll buggy, the very young girl took action. "I went to the bank and deposited. Didn't know how to do it. Went there myself.

Didn't tell mama and them I was goin'. . . . I commenced to save money. I never would take any of it out. I just put it in. . . . It's not the ones that make the big money, but the ones who know how to save who get ahead. You got to leave it alone long enough for it to increase."

Increase it did. According to the article, "When she retired in 1995, her hands painfully swollen with arthritis, this washerwoman who had been paid in little piles of coins and dollar bills her entire life had $280,000 in the bank." She promptly donated $150,000 of that to the University of Southern Mississippi, to help needy students attend college.

Forgoing consumption and saving one's money ultimately leads to having assets to invest. It's not easy in an era of mass advertising and ubiquitous consumption. But Oseola McCarty had another insight. "Hard work gives your life meaning," she said. "Everyone needs to work hard at somethin' to feel good about themselves. Every job can be done well and every day has its satisfactions. . . . If you want to feel proud of yourself, you've got to do things you can be proud of."

Pride in a job well done is a great reward. It's a good starting point for valuing work over consumption. I remember Mr. E showing me how to wash a car. He really cared that I learn to do it right (with circular scrubbing and a lot of elbow grease!). Or the time Mr. E made a bet with our housekeeper over who could wring more water out of a rag. He was intent on squeezing out every last drop, not to let any go to waste. He lost. But I'll never forget that lesson. After his Coke story, it took me about twenty years to ever spring for a soft drink at a meal, and I still can't get used to it!

Thrift may be making a comeback with the millennial generation, the cohort that came of age after the year 2000. They had to grow up watching the tech bubble burst, September 11, the Iraq war, and the Great Recession. They are saddled with enormous amounts of student debt. In some ways, their experience echoes that of the generation that grew up during the Great Depression. The millennial generation places more value on experiences than material objects, which is hopeful. Like Oseola McCarty, they are finding meaning in their own way. "My secret was contentment. I was happy with what I had," said McCarty.

Time

Time has a number of positive attributes for the investor. It can be a catalyst in patient investments. It gives you negotiating leverage. It gives you option value. Time reveals the distinction between a cyclical trend, a passing fancy, and a meaningful secular direction. In many of the best investments, time is your partner.

As our industry has become more and more obsessed with measuring IRR, time is increasingly seen as the enemy. Mathematically, time lowers your return for the same economics. With the advent of instant communications and spreadsheets that can calculate your returns down to the day, everyone seems to be in a rush.

Real estate is a slow business that isn't suited to rushing. Neighborhoods and cities mature over time. Old, below-market leases roll, offering the opportunity to raise rents. Assembling the land, plans, entitlements, and materials to build a great building also requires patience. Rome was not built in a day. Or in the words of the Roman emperor Augustus, who got a fair amount done: *Festina lente.* Make haste slowly.

We were once offered an unbelievable piece of land on the ocean in Surfside, Florida, not far from the world-famous Bal Harbour Shops. The area was on the upswing. One hundred feet of beach frontage and unobstructed Atlantic Ocean views, just like 321 Ocean. The price seemed too good to be true, and it was. There was a coop built on it with thirty-five years left on the lease. The monthly rent payments of only $6,000 a year were locked in until the 2040s!

I recalled my job interview after business school with Seth Klarman. Seth had asked me to consider a thought experiment—how to choose between two investments that had the same high IRR. The most straightforward answer, at the heart of finance, is the one that is less risky. For the same high return, you'd rather take less risk. I'd also choose the bigger one. All else being equal, you'd rather hit your home run on a large investment than on a small one.

Seth told me there was a third answer. Here I really had to think hard, which in itself made the interview life-changing for me. Then it hit me. For the same high IRR, an investment that lasts longer is better. It's really hard to generate high returns. Doing so consistently over a long period of time is the key to successful investing. A short-term pop makes fewer absolute dollars than a great long-term investment. We are so conditioned by the frenetic pace of business—and by the time value of money as captured in IRR—that it's easy to forget that time can be our friend.

Armed with Klarman's insight, we jumped on the Surfside opportunity. Leased fee interests—parcels of land that someone has leased for many years—present some of the best underappreciated values in real estate. They're often archaeological relics from another era, rented well below market. When the lease was written some fifty or seventy-five years ago, a dollar was worth much more. If the landlord wasn't careful, as in the Surfside example, inflation would erode the value of their lease cash flows. But the land itself should be inflation proof. All you have to do is wait for the lease to expire or reset, and you get a huge bump up in cash flow. The simple passage of time is your catalyst. That's one catalyst I can usually muster a fair degree of confidence in!

In the Surfside deal, we also got wind that a developer was in advanced negotiations with the Four Seasons to build a five-star hotel three doors down. That would be a game changer. But the deal was complicated. We weren't buying the whole thing. The land was owned fifty-fifty between a brother and a sister in an archaic ownership structure. You guessed it . . . tenants-in-common! It was the broken vase. Déjà vu all over again. It was the same thesis that kept reappearing in different forms, the Brooklyn Bar Menu Generator in action.

My partner David engaged in shuttle diplomacy, working night and day to reunite the property. The two siblings were in litigation and hadn't talked in years while the property languished. It was a depressing dynamic, but David found a way to make both parties happy. We bought the two 50 percent interests and continue to hold the land. Every day that passes is a day closer to realizing the full land value of several times the purchase price. *Festina lente*!

Institutional constraints around time often preclude the big guys from competing with you for long-term investments like Surfside. This smacks of illiquidity and a good value investment opportunity. If something is worth two, three, or ten times more vacant than you are paying today, the risk of losing money is *de minimis*. All you have to do is let time elapse. Which it tends to do!

Negotiations

Negotiations are both essential and constant in real estate investment. But the alternative is worse! Thoughtful and creative negotiation can help uncover what people value more than money, and lay the groundwork for value investment.

Litigation appeared imminent as negotiations on William Street ground to a halt. We had sold the property where I had learned the ropes of development to a self-made billionaire, Tamir Sapir, who was represented by his son and his attorney. To get a good price in the sale, we had offered financing to the buyer, as it was a large project. We had done a ton of architectural work and commenced excavation on the development, and were to be reimbursed by the buyer based on a fixed value of the land. Then it turned out that the site might have archaeological significance. It might have been the site of a Revolutionary War–era tavern, with a well into which inebriated local Dutchmen and English traders tossed their pints of ale. Work stopped for several months while historians established the facts.

This time cost Sapir a lot of money and increased the uncertainty of the project. He wanted to reconsider, and his son felt that he had been treated unfairly. The train seemed to be going off the rails. Then Uncle Fred came up with an unconventional approach. "You be the judge," he told Sapir. "Whatever you decide is fair is what we will do." This seemed nuts. Why give your counterpart in a negotiation full power over the outcome? They could choose anything. Yet instead of commencing costly litigation, Sapir decided on a fair number.

It was a great, old-fashioned solution that represents the way traditional real estate players work. Instead of running to court, they work it out. And Uncle Fred's gamble paid off, because it was based on mutual respect. Sapir felt empowered as the judge and jury of the situation, and could not rely on any base instinct of more is better. He felt honor-bound to do the right thing. Fred anticipated this and saved the day.

Dollars and cents are rarely the key to a negotiation. Much more powerful are the human elements of pride, shame, honor, status, friendship, fairness, and reciprocity. In a negotiation, the key is to figure out what makes the other parties tick, and what they need to get out of a mess. Essentially, it's empathy, seeing yourself in the other party's shoes—no matter how mad you may be at them at that moment!

Often what people ask for isn't what they need. They may ask for money, or demand that you do something specific. But there's often a human story behind the bluster. Have they been slighted? Are they a bully, or a good person who has been misunderstood? To find a solution to the financial equation, you have to understand what the underlying human problem is.

The other half of negotiation is understanding yourself. What makes *you* tick? Are you quick to anger, or do you have the patience of a saint? Do you come across as accommodating or intimidating? Do you crave affirmation or victory or peace of mind? If you know the mistakes and biases you bring to the table, you'll be better able to come up with creative solutions.

One thing I've found in every phase of my career is that it is important to stand up for yourself. You can do this in a humble and kind and authentic way. But never give in to bullies. You will be unsatisfied. Bullies need to be stood up to. They often can't handle a taste of their own medicine. Sometimes they are genuinely surprised to learn that they are being a jerk.

The conventional wisdom is that confronting powerful, arrogant, important people will just make them angrier. Let it go. But if they see that you mean business and can stand up for yourself, they'll have much more respect for you. On countless occasions, confronting what I perceived as bullying has led to a much better working relationship. Occasionally even a friendship.

A reputation for honor is a huge asset in any negotiation. As we saw in the case of Uncle Fred and Tamir Sapir, it's much easier to solve complex problems if there's a baseline of trust. You can propose innovative solutions, and people will believe in you to follow through. There's almost always a partial win-win somewhere, if not a full one.

Mr. E was trained in the bazaars of Tehran, Tabriz, and Istanbul buying and selling antiques. There the strategy is to build relationships over many years, so you can trust the authenticity of the merchandise. You sit for a cup of tea and take your time. You beat around the bush and are always polite. You start with a very low offer, and the other person starts with a very high number. Eventually you get close enough to see if there's a deal to be made. If the other person doesn't seem to be reasonable, you can always politely take your leave and see if it's a bluff.

This school of negotiation is no less applicable today. If you are in a rush, you rarely have negotiating leverage. Conversely, taking your time if the other person is pushing hard quickly turns the tables on them. It's tough to do because we are impatient. We naturally want to get things done and take care of business. But that can be a weakness in negotiation.

The most effective aid in negotiation is competition. It's the equivalent of walking out of the shop in the bazaar. You can say you'd love to buy these beautiful floors from this vendor whom you know to be reputable, but you have a lower offer; can we meet in the middle? Doing the work to find out what your alternatives are is the best way to establish a strong negotiating position. You can try bluffing that you have a great alternative, but beware—the other party may call your bluff!

It's best to be aware of who you are negotiating with and their position. Negotiating the price of a building or the cost of construction is totally reasonable if it's done at the appropriate time in the right way. Just don't crush a guy who depends on that job to put food on the table that night. If they really need the extra cents to get by, and it's a fair price for the goods or services, I don't feel the need to negotiate.

In the real estate business, you are sometimes negotiating with people who have a lot less power than you do. It might be an impoverished tenant who has nowhere else to live, or a laborer who badly needs that paycheck. In those cases, I prefer to let them win. I don't want to win those negotiations. I'd rather negotiate hard with equals who can carry their own weight, or people in a stronger position than myself. That feels more honorable in a Robin Hood sense.

I don't believe in renegotiating a deal once someone has trusted you and you've agreed on a price. I believe a handshake is a handshake. Those who shave a few pennies off a contract by negotiating with a tradesman who has already done the work, and therefore has no leverage left, are abusing their power and trust. If the work is truly faulty, give them a chance to fix it.

Because real estate is at its heart a privately negotiated business, in the sense that it is not traded on an exchange, not to negotiate is to put yourself at a disadvantage. Negotiating in an honorable and authentic way is a key part of value investment in real estate. Building a reputation and trust is very much the way of traditional real estate.

Negotiating styles are deeply rooted in many cultures, because they get to the heart of fundamental cultural values—fairness, hospitality, trust, honor, and betrayal. Because real estate in global cities is such an international business, it's important to be aware of where your negotiating partner is coming from. Are they from Moscow, where smiling makes you look foolish, or Tehran, where a smile accompanies the toughest medicine? Do they hail from Minneapolis, where being a straight shooter builds trust, or Shanghai, where it's impolite to say no? Each culture brings its own choreography of negotiation.

When I wanted to propose to my wife, Eva, I got an unexpected taste of Persian negotiations. I decided to meet her father and ask for her hand in marriage. Little did I know that in Persian tradition a father is supposed to play hard to get, and politeness requires him to give you a run for your money.

I went in and earnestly put my cards on the table—I was in love and wanted to marry his daughter. No response. Just a cup of tea and a thorough grilling on my plans for the future and how well I appreciated his daughter's special qualities. Then my future in-laws invited me to stay for dinner with no final answer. I was expecting a clear "yea" or "nay" vote like in Congress, and I got a filibuster. After two hours I left with a good feeling . . . but no clear answer. The joke was on me. I was supposed to conduct a full-blown negotiation to win her hand!

The Deep Structure
of Investing

There is a common thread running through the one hundred most frequently used words in the English language. It's not their length. It's not the subject matter. Marinate for a while and see if it comes to you what that common denominator is. It subtly underlies the structure of our communications each day.

I believe that the deep structures that underlie wise investment and real estate are analogous to those in language. They are a powerful organizing force below the surface. We have discussed how patterns of illiquidity underlie the best investments. If you can find those, you can find out what makes a potential value investment. Understanding the deeper structures of investing comes gradually, through trial and error, and seeing the same situations reappear throughout history.

This structural way of thinking began to resonate with me during my time as a financial analyst at Credit Suisse First Boston after college. It accelerated when I was able to compare and contrast my work in the Mergers & Acquisitions Group with that in the Principal Transactions Group, which was using the bank's own capital to invest in real estate debt. M&A was boot camp for poring over financial statements. The key was getting at the quantitative truth of how a company was doing to inform its proper valuation (hint: the good stuff is usually in the footnotes!). One managing director at the firm, the one who espoused management by fear, once plunked a statistics textbook on my desk and demanded a full statistical analysis of limited-float public companies—by tomorrow morning.

The Principal Transactions Group presented a different kind of challenge. The group was headed by Andy Stone of *Liar's Poker* fame, a guru of converting real estate into bonds as commercial mortgage-backed securities (CMBS). He was a really great boss. We sat on a huge open floor, and I sat closest to the trading desk. This meant that I could see the back-and-forth between the bankers who were making real estate loans and the bond traders. They were relaying information about the implied pricing required to make a profit on converting the loans into bonds.

Bond people are often quietly the smartest people in the room, which makes them very dangerous. These guys had reinvented finance over the previous twenty years. Sitting between the bankers and the traders gave me a perfect perch to understand the heart of the financial system—intermediation between sources and uses of capital. It illustrated how you could transform illiquid real estate loans into bonds. It was a fascinating lesson in investment, if you didn't get hit by a thrown telephone or caught up in one of the pranks that are a big part of Wall Street lore. After a particularly rough prank, one analyst challenged an associate to a boxing match, which occurred in a ring at one of the city's old boxing gyms. The whole floor showed up to cheer them on. As the singer of the group, I was enlisted to sing the national anthem before the match!

I was stationed with Dean Cederquist, the brilliant deal guy and jazz saxophonist. Dean's job was to focus on making credit tenant loans, mortgages secured by real estate that's been leased to credit-worthy corporate tenants for a long time. These are a cash-flowing, corporate equivalent of the Surfside deal. I was enlisted because I had just spent one hundred hours a week on corporate financial analysis. If your property is leased for twenty years to Home Depot, Walgreens, Motel 6, or a Pennsylvania health system, you'd better be sure your tenant is creditworthy!

It was a fascinating mix of real estate and corporate bonds. Bonds because you were measuring the risks of a company's credit. Real estate because when the lease ran out, or if anything happened to the tenant, you owned the property vacant. While the credit of the tenant was paramount, you had better like the real estate too!

The ideal credit tenant lease was one that was "bondable." This meant that all of the messy obligations of real estate ownership were borne by the corporate tenant, so the real estate could easily be turned into bonds. If the building burned down, the tenant had to have insurance to fix it. Same if the property was condemned and taken by the state. If the roof caved in, the tenant was responsible. It was basically, don't call me, just send a check—the equivalent of a corporate bond. That meant that you could focus primarily on the bond-like aspects of the property, the cash flows, and their credit-worthiness. The real estate was largely an afterthought.

Credit tenant deals are a kind of a perfect square of real estate, a simpler structure with fewer variables that lets you understand how real estate works. Vacancy is zero, and the tenant's credit can be analyzed. This takes two of the biggest complexities out of the equation. What's left are two archetypal parts of real estate: a bond and raw land.

Understanding the important structures underlying real estate can help you understand the dizzying array of real estate investments that come your way. They aren't always front and center, but their subtle effects can be very powerful.

The common denominator of the one hundred most commonly used words is that they all descend from the Anglo-Saxon language of the Germanic tribes that invaded England some 1,500 years ago. England was conquered in 1066 by French-speaking Vikings from Normandy. Half of modern English vocabulary derives from French, Latin, or other Romance languages. But today we still largely speak the tribal language that became Old English. All one hundred of our most common words in twenty-first-century America descend from this ancient tongue.

Words, like buildings or bonds, are powerful tools that we use every day. But the logic of their structure and organization often lies below the surface.

Parallel Structures

Variants of this underlying structure would pop up again and again throughout my career like musical variations on a theme. Appreciating what made each case unique and what remained constant between them was a great teacher. The structure reappeared in a discounted zero-coupon form in the Surfside leased fee investment. A variant of the same bond-like story appeared in Gotham Center in Long Island City. The project was leased to New York City for twenty years, so the credit of the tenant was one thing you didn't need to worry too much about. (Well, in 2008 you had to worry about everything, including municipal credit ratings!)

It came back in my first deal at Square Mile that I had tackled while finishing business school. We were shown some defaulted CMBS bonds backed by a pool of loans against distribution centers for the supermarket chain Winn-Dixie. Unfortunately for the landlord of the space, and the holder of the bonds, Winn-Dixie had filed for bankruptcy. Defaulted loans on the far-flung warehouses of a bankrupt supermarket chain were not the sexiest real estate investment! But they were trading at a big discount. Just as I had a crash course in statistics in my job at Credit Suisse First Boston, this deal required a crash course in bankruptcy law to understand its financial structure. It forced me to draw upon an understanding of the archetypal components of real estate investment, the underlying structure of risk and reward.

Reasoning by analogy to the other credit leased deals I had faced, I figured you could break down the value of the investment into three parts: 1) bonds, in the form of my familiar credit

tenant loans to a reorganized Winn-Dixie, with additional security in the mission-critical warehouses they elected to hold on to,
2) pure real estate in the form of the vacant warehouses that they
rejected in bankruptcy, and 3) shares of stock in the company. By
looking closely at each of the different pieces, we were able to identify that the sum of the parts was worth more than the price of the
defaulted bonds.

Analyzing a distressed credit tenant deal, the perfect square
of real estate, offered a unique window into the nature of risk and
reward. We could see each component of value, and the various
risks of real estate, spread out before our eyes. It was like one of
the prisms in Mr. E's homemade crystal chandeliers that bends light
and spreads it to reveal red, orange, and yellow, green, blue, indigo,
and violet. In clear, unbroken light, all of those colors are there, but
you can't see them.

In newly created or happily leased real estate, all of the components of risk are there, but hidden, like DNA that subtly guides
human development over the course of years. Could we use an
understanding of the end of the movie—the distressed Winn-Dixie
bonds—to better understand the characters at the beginning, the
latent risk and reward underlying real estate? Yes. It took financial
distress and the bankruptcy process to elucidate the risks that were
lurking but poorly understood.

When I was at HBS, I took a particularly intriguing finance
class with Professor Peter Tufano, who is now dean of Oxford's
Business School. Tufano showed us how to break down any investment into its constituent parts, the molecules that make up the
whole. He invited us to look at an investment as a combination of
risk-free bonds, risky bonds, risky assets, and options—the fundamental archetypes of risk and reward in finance. It was reminiscent
of the nineteenth-century painter Cézanne, who foreshadowed

twentieth-century modern art with his contention that all of space could be expressed in spheres, cylinders, and cones!

If you understood how the risks and rewards worked for each simple part, you could deduce how the whole would behave under various conditions, both logically and mathematically. It was a powerful way to analyze risk and reward, one that rang true with my comparative approach honed in credit tenant lease deals. Using this method, every deal you do can be another piece in the puzzle of understanding.

Transforming real estate into bonds, and seeing bonds transformed back into real estate through financial distress, was like seeing ice melted into water and then frozen again. It laid bare some of the transformations of liquidity that are at the heart of finding real value. The distress of the Winn-Dixie bonds revealed underlying structures that were there all along. And Tufano's method is a powerful framework. For me, grappling with theory and practice yielded an understanding of pure forms that can be applied to many different deals. It revealed a glimpse of the deep structure of real estate investing. Real estate is by nature part bond and part land. No wonder it takes both value investment and traditional real estate to fully appreciate this deep craft!

Risk

I learned a few other things about how things can go wrong as well. June 2, 1999, was a placid day at the Ocean Trails Golf Course, which was preparing for its grand opening on July Fourth weekend. It was a development fifty years in the making, starting when the developer's father bought a garbanzo bean farm sloping alongside the Pacific Ocean in Rancho Palos Verdes, California. After the town opened a brief window for development, it had been a ten-year slog through town planning and environmental permitting to develop a Pete Dye golf course and residential community. But all that hard work was about to pay off. Credit Suisse First Boston, where I was working at that time, was the lender on the project.

Suddenly, without warning, the fairway of the eighteenth hole plunged into the Pacific Ocean. Seventeen acres of land slid into the water, leaving a gaping chasm surrounded by swirling eddies. To add insult to injury, the eighteenth hole itself remained above water, accessible only by helicopter or grappling hook! Who should pay for the repairs? Was it the responsibility of the insurance company, the municipality with an old sewer line that may have been leaking, or no one but the developer? Thankfully, no one was hurt in the mudslide. But it became a long legal battle and a financial disaster for the developer and lender.

From the outside, investing in real estate looks like a simple solution to the risk the world throws at you. Everyone loves the idea of real estate because you're buying something tangible. The truth is, if you've been around long enough, you've seen the fortunes of many highfliers dashed on the rocks of recessions. You've seen the bitter fruits of interest rate fluctuations, tax policies, technological changes, credit crises, leverage, and often enough, hubris. Unfortunately, real estate doesn't come with a warning label that tells you whether it's risky or not. As the old joke goes, the quickest way to make a small fortune in real estate is to start with a large one.

In my own career, I've seen real estate fortunes reversed by the Asian crisis, the Russian crisis, the Fed takeover of Long-Term Capital Management, devaluations in Brazil and Argentina, hyperinflation and the chaos of formerly Communist countries trying capitalism and democracy and then authoritarianism. I've witnessed coups, the tech bubble, September 11, the Iraq war, deindustrialization, Hurricane Katrina, the housing bubble, the credit crunch, and Hurricane Sandy. Then came the Great Recession, the foreclosure crisis, extraordinary monetary stimulus, quantitative easing, the collapse of oil prices, the rise of the dollar, the retail apocalypse, and many other smaller crises. Just looking at the successful real estate investors of today isn't the right way to see risk; it is skewed by survivorship bias. In retrospect, if the deals work out, investing in real estate looks easy. If not, you are often out of business!

I have an obsession with risk, and it has been a deep part of my investing. I don't know anyone who cares as much. Some of this comes to me from Mr. E, who was incredibly risk-averse. Thanks to a cautious, conservative approach, he survived the deep downturns of the 1970s and 1990s, and his successors survived the Great Recession without a hitch. Some of that rubbed off on me.

I recently heard a story that cast some light on the origins of Mr. E's worldview, that for better or worse he passed on to me.

In 1892, a group of Jewish citizens of the town of Hamadan in Persia were distraught. One man, Lalezari, was the grandson of the most learned and respected Jewish leader in all of Persia. He had received diplomats from Europe and had a library filled with philosophical, scientific, and religious texts. Hamadan had been a center of Jewish life in Iran for over 2,500 years, and a local edifice is revered as the Tomb of Esther and Mordechai. All of the men had faced increased harassment by the local religious authorities.

One of the local leaders, Mullah Abdollah, was a cruel man who decided to punish the Jews of his town. He began enforcing anti-quated laws that had been on the books since the Safavid dynasty, when the rulers of Iran sought to establish Shiism as the law of the land. These included such draconian measures as refusing to sell food to Jews because of their ritual impurity, and preventing Jews from going out in the rain because they might dirty their Islamic neighbors.

According to an 1892 report in the *Bulletin of the Alliance Israélite Universelle*, "Many of the Jews had come under house arrest and life had become virtually intolerable. Nursing babies died of starvation in their mother's arms as their mother's milk had dried up." With power slipping from the hands of the decadent Qajar dynasty in Tehran, Mullah Abdollah had a free rein to run Hama-dan. The Jewish community asked the Shah in Tehran for help. The Shah sent troops to try to regain control of the city, but they were repulsed by an angry mob led by Abdollah. Even the head of the Hamadan Constabulary was forced to kiss Mullah Abdollah's feet for daring to try to pacify his angry mob.

On the eve of Yom Kippur in September of 1892, Lalezari and his community were at their wits' end. An angry mob whipped up by Abdollah was rampaging though the Jewish Quarter. Lalezari and a group of thirty other Jews headed to the telegraph agency to see if they could contact the authorities in Tehran or foreign repre-sentatives, anyone who might be able to rein in the cruel caprices of Abdollah. As they stood in the telegraph agency, they heard sounds of the mob approaching and barricaded the doors. They did every-thing to keep the fanatical crowd from tearing down the doors, fearing a certain massacre. But to no avail! The doors were broken down and the mob entered and surrounded the Jewish men. They were held at sword point and forced to convert to Islam or die on the spot.

Lalezari was Mr. E's grandfather. For me, this is risk.

Mr. E never told me that story. He loved America and the opportunity he found here. He never wanted to look back. But I believe growing up with a taste of this world had a big impact on how he built his life in the real estate business. It gave him the guts to leave everything and start fresh in America. And it impacted how he wanted to invest—with honor and dignity, without wasting a penny, avoiding risk. After living through perilous times and sailing to America for opportunity, he saw investment as building safety and security for his family.

Learning how to invest is like walking through a field where bullets are whizzing by you. Risk is the front line in the epic battle between bravery and prudence. For my taste, people don't pay enough attention to risk. Most finance people in real estate obsess about reward. They build models to count their chickens. And they measure risk in ways that I find misleading. Mine is a visceral, tribal, historic understanding of risk, one that is very different from what is taught in business schools across the country today.

The discipline of investing means studying history to overcome risk and find security in a capricious world. If you focus too much on reward, you forget about risk and you get burned. If you focus on risk, the reward usually takes care of itself. As the value investor Larry Tisch put it, "Once you've eliminated the possibility of losing money, all the other options are good!"

Leverage

Mr. E had a clear view on leverage. He avoided it whenever possible. He and his brothers would celebrate when they were able to tear up a mortgage. There is actually a property that he made my father promise never to mortgage. This way it would be there through thick or thin. This is a far cry from how people utilize leverage in real estate today.

Excessive leverage dramatically increases the risk of losing money. No matter how high the intrinsic value of your asset, if you are short on liquidity to refinance a maturing loan, you're in trouble. You will be at the mercy of the temporarily prevailing subjective market value, not the true value of your asset.

As the market gets hotter, people borrow more and more with shorter and shorter term. This increases the risk that at the moment of truth, the market may hold a different opinion of value than you do. In those cases, if you're overleveraged, the market wins. As the famous economist John Maynard Keynes apocryphally stated, "Markets can remain irrational longer than you can remain solvent."

One of the classic examples of leverage magnifying risk was the failure of Long-Term Capital Management in the late 1990s. Long-Term Capital was one of the first hedge funds, and used copious amounts of leverage to amplify small bets on the direction of a particular stock or bond. It was run by two Nobel Prize–winning economists who had practically founded the field of financial economics. The source of their downfall was actually an interesting value investment. But it was doomed by leverage mismatch.

They noticed that certain Asian closed-end funds were trading for less than the value of the individual stocks that they owned. Mathematically, they were absolutely correct. There was no reason for the anomaly to persist. But they used enormous amounts of leverage to magnify the impact of their ingenious bet. For whatever reason, the value gap didn't close. Markets remained irrational longer than they could stay solvent. The company had to be bailed out by the New York Fed.

Seeing two Nobel Prize winners fail spectacularly, even when they had a value investment thesis, was a true lesson in humility. If it could happen to them, it could surely happen to me.

When I went to work for a bank in mergers and acquisitions after college, Mr. E was a bit baffled. To be fair, I truly had very little idea what investment banking was either. My uncle Henry told me that their grandfather had been a "banker" in Persia. With a laugh he explained that that meant that he sat cross-legged on the floor in front of a huge safe while studying the Torah. Kurdish shepherds would give him a few coins for safekeeping while they went on their nomadic journeys. Perhaps I shouldn't have been surprised that this bore little resemblance to investment banking as practiced in late-twentieth-century America.

Mr. E had his own idea of what banking was, which he shared over some Persian lunch specials when I could escape from my office to meet him. Banking was conservative, prized safety, and never espoused risk—like my friend Andrew Brody at JPMorgan, who has never lost money on a loan. He's been pitching a no-hitter since the 1980s.

On my graduation from college, Mr. E gave me a few stock certificates in a company called CoreStates Financial that he had been keeping for me in a safe. Some twenty years before, he had met the representatives of a bank in Philadelphia. He liked their management, which surely meant they were sufficiently risk-averse. He bought a few shares. Then they were acquired by another bank, and another bank, and so forth, until they became CoreStates Financial.

Mr. E didn't live to see the company abandon caution. They merged with First Union and then Wachovia and drowned in a sea of bad debt. Somewhere along this journey, banks had lost the conservative values of lending and investing that had so impressed Mr. E in Philadelphia.

During my time in banking in 1998, Russia defaulted on its bonds. After nearly a decade of cowboy capitalism, shock therapy, and dysfunctional government, the country could not meet its obligations. Its bonds dropped in price as the spreads over treasuries, the extra interest investors demanded to hold a risky asset, catapulted upward. But not just Russian bonds, all emerging market bonds. And then many United States bonds dropped in price as their credit spreads also widened. This included CMBS.

The bank was sitting on a huge inventory of loans secured by high-quality real estate. These were the raw materials that were to be converted into bonds. But after the Russian crisis, the market demanded a higher risk premium on all bonds. The value of CMBS took a hit, and with it all the inventory of real estate loans on the books. It was like a merchant caught holding inventory when all the competition goes on sale. For reasons unconnected to real estate, the value of a ton of the bank's real estate–related debt instruments tanked. It was a painful lesson in how risk can come from unexpected quarters. It was a credit crunch and in a sense a dress rehearsal of what was to come.

As with the Winn-Dixie mortgage bonds, it often takes financial distress to understand the true nature of things. When the economy is good, we forget about the leverage upon which the system rests. But in bad times it becomes readily apparent. As value investors like to say, "When the tide goes out, we'll see who's swimming naked."

In the credit crunch and subprime crisis of 2007, I witnessed a strikingly parallel collapse to what had roiled CMBS markets during the Russian crisis. Liquidity evaporated. Structures that seemed sound were revealed to be overleveraged. Seen through the analytical framework of pure structural forms that I had learned in Professor Tufano's class, it began to look as if everything was a leveraged bond fund. Everything was comprised of leverage upon leverage.

And not just CMBS. Almost all of the financial sector is built on leverage upon leverage. Banks are leveraged 95 to 98 percent. They are not normal companies. They are basically a portfolio of loans and bonds leveraged to the hilt. They are for all intents and purposes CMBS, just not limited to real estate. As the crisis unfolded, it also became apparent that insurance companies are leveraged bond funds. They invest in bonds, loans, and real estate and are financed by future obligations to policyholders. Only when credit markets freeze up do people recognize the degree of leverage in the financial system.

Real estate too can be looked at as a leveraged bond fund. An office building pools together streams of cash flows from a variety of tenants of differing creditworthiness, and consolidates them into a net operating income that can be used to obtain leverage. Leverage is embedded everywhere in real estate, from financial leverage to operating leverage to the latent leverage intrinsic to land investments. In my view, land holds an implied kernel of leverage the way a caterpillar contains a butterfly. You need leverage to construct the asset on it and generate cash flows, so in a sense the land is leveraged real estate in chrysalis form.

The notion that huge chunks of the financial sector are essentially analogous to CMBS is not a reassuring one. But it gives you a sense of how big segments of the economy behave under certain conditions. Under stress, as in the example of the Winn-Dixie bonds, the true colors of your real estate are revealed. The same applies more broadly in finance. When the going gets tough, everything is a leveraged bond fund. An awareness of embedded leverage, and leverage upon leverage, is critical. You can't avoid leverage entirely. The key is to understand it and how it impacts your business, and to use it parsimoniously and wisely to your advantage.

Experience in the credit markets, whether as a lender or working out bad loans, makes you a better investor. From Vista 12 to the Winn-Dixie bonds, we have found many opportunities by acquiring debt. Having spent time on both sides of the coin, I think a lot of equity guys would benefit from thinking more like distressed debt guys, and vice versa. Being a lender or working out bad real estate deals forces you to grapple constantly with the prospect of loss. This kind of downside focus is both a trait of character and your strongest suit analytically. A wise real estate investor studies both debt and equity to find rewards without taking too much risk.

The ancient Jewish scholar Hillel once had a student who was in a hurry. The student asked Hillel to teach him all the wisdom of the Bible while he was standing on one foot. Hillel told him a variation on the Golden Rule—"Do not do to your neighbor that which is hateful to you." *The Omnivore's Dilemma*, a terrific book on food, breaks it down like this: "Eat everything. Mostly plants." Here's my version: "Buy great real estate cheaply. Without too much leverage."

Value Investment Transformation— Illiquidity to Liquidity

We have seen powerful cases where the sudden drying up of liquidity causes catastrophe. The opposite, when the dams break and liquidity comes streaming in, unlocks great value in real estate. Sometimes this transformation is epic in scale. Other times, you can achieve it in your deal.

The transformation from illiquidity to liquidity is momentous when it happens in large scale. It can be driven by the spread of capitalism bringing illiquid sectors of the economy into a market-based system. In my banking days, I saw entire industries change as conglomerates or stagnant corporations were reorganized into more dynamic enterprises. I saw the privatization of state-owned companies unleash a wave of market liquidity across Europe, the Eastern Bloc, and the developing world in the 1990s. The change from illiquidity to liquidity is an inflection point worth paying attention to.

My favorite real estate professor, Arthur Segel, is a visionary who saw these changes coming and found a way to become a part of them. In his US investment business, Professor Segel found value buying office buildings "with a story," where reduced liquidity created a buying opportunity. This is the strategy I have tried to follow. By turning around the asset and resolving the idiosyncratic issues clouding its marketability, he was able to realize the value locked in the illiquidity. Over several decades, this liquidity story writ large through public and private markets has led to broadly higher valuations in US real estate.

Professor Segel saw the signs of a similar pattern emerging in India in the 2000s. The partial deregulation of real estate development presaged enormous changes in an industry long closed to outside investment and starved of capital. A change in laws made a market where there was none. Like a dam bursting, the flow of capital and the introduction of liquidity was a catalyst for the realization of value in that vibrant society and economy. In many ways this change recapitulated the transformation of the US real estate market. It went from a scrappy operating business into an institutional asset class over the last few decades. Note to self: whenever a large swath of an important world economy introduces liquidity where there had been none, it's worth a hard look.

The individual real estate deals we have looked at offer a microcosm of these epic transformations, from special situations to liquidity. They take you from one archetypal part of real estate investment, land, to another—bond-like liquidity.

If you seek to marry value investment with traditional real estate values, you have to be intrepid in finding challenging situations that yield unexpected value. That means finding broken, complex deals. But it also means exploring private or public markets, debt or equity, direct ownership or partnership interests. You have to be willing to go wherever necessary to buy great real estate for a good price.

This journey requires a catalyst to help you get from point A to point B. There are two types of catalysts in real estate investing. If you've worked hard and buy right, a catalyst may materialize simply through the passage of time. Rossini's librettist captured this dynamic memorably in *The Barber of Seville*, with the phrase "the cheese just fell on the Macaroni!" That's when someone builds a Four Seasons or a museum or a transportation hub next door to you. It's when a long-term below-market lease expires after you've waited patiently for many years. In value investment, the cheese sometimes falls on the macaroni—usually after a lot of hard work and careful analysis.

You can fill the vacancy, as Cousin Greg did. You can figure out the underlying dynamic of a neighborhood and get in at a good basis. Then the evolution of the location can be a catalyst for the realization of your value thesis. With the passage of time, there's always the chance the cheese will fall, that the hard work of others will make you look like a genius. You don't underwrite it, you don't plan it, you just buy right and position yourself well. You may have earned the privilege of being pleasantly surprised.

Real estate rarely offers you such passive options. The tools required are usually more along the lines of a famous scene in Puccini's *La Bohème*. The young poet Rodolfo gets a visit from his neighbor Mimi. She has come to his apartment because her candle has blown out. She drops her key and they stumble around in the dark looking for it. When Rodolfo suddenly finds it, he pretends to still be looking so she won't leave! Then their hands touch. The rest is history. Reminiscing about how they fell in love, Rodolfo sings "*aiutavo il destino*," I helped destiny.

In real estate, destiny usually needs a little push! You have to reimagine, transform, or create your investment from the ground up. After we bought 321 Ocean from two banks, made a deal with forty-nine tenants to redevelop The Clifton, and restructured Vista 12, we had to physically transform the properties to realize the special value they held. That work is real estate development. It is a calling that draws upon every fiber of your being. Development is a journey you take with land from illiquidity into liquidity. That's a journey I want to take.

The Handshake Philosophy

On January 19, 1999, my grandfather Eskandar, Mr. E, passed away. For me, it was the loss of a true friend and the end of an era. I was heartbroken. I was lucky enough to spend some time with him beforehand. We decided to take a road trip through California together upon my graduation from college. We drove from Los Angeles to Joshua Tree to Palm Springs, staying in the finest roadside budget hotels we could find. First, we visited Mr. E's sister and our cousins who had settled in LA and still lived in a Persian world with delicious food. Years later, when brother and sister were on their deathbeds, they each instructed us not to tell the other. In their true soulful fashion, neither sibling wanted the other to know they were suffering.

Then we set out over the mountains and into the desert, a landscape my grandfather loved. As a city kid, I wasn't so sure behind the wheel, but he helped me drive over every ridge. I had made a tape of some of his favorite songs from records, and he explained what they meant. In particular we both loved a romantic song "Mara Beboos," which tells the story of a father saying goodbye to his daughter. Legend has it that the song was written by a prisoner due to be executed the next day. It reminded me of one of my favorite songs, "Danny Boy," an Irish song sung to a lover who's going off to war. And Puccini's "Ch'ella mi creda" that was adopted by Italian soldiers going off to World War I. "Let her believe that I am free and far away," the singer implores. It's a song of emotional generosity and farewell.

We found we were continuously passing creeks and dried-out riverbeds as we drove through the mountains back to the coast to go home. Mr. E explained that highways were often built along rivers because that was where the land was the flattest—where eons of trickling streams had cut a path through the mountains. That was an eye-opener. His appreciation of nature and land was visceral and based in love and life experience.

When I went to visit him in the hospital years later, his condition was deteriorating rapidly. He could no longer speak to express his emotions or to say goodbye. Then he took my hand and kissed it. It was one of the most primal, powerful gestures of my life, and I knew exactly what it meant.

The burial was on an ice-cold winter day with freezing snow in the grass. There were several moving eulogies. I remember vividly one by my aunt Zaza that recalled my grandfather's favorite plants and flowers that created the landscape in which his love was so palpable. Gardenias, lily of the valley, mint, honeysuckle.

One memory that stood out was a handwritten letter from an older Polish lady who was truly moved by his passing. She wanted to thank him and express her gratitude for having given her a job fifty years earlier.

I met a man who had done business with Mr. E in 1969. It was a simple deal, but it left an imprint. Some forty years later, this man still remembered Mr. E as a gentleman who had kept his word and honored his handshake.

Real estate investment gives you the power to take structures that are broken and render them whole, unlocking value in the process. You can take vacancy, waste, raw materials, and the illiquid detritus of past eras and transform them into something beautiful, cash-flowing, and liquid. And you can do it with courage, patience, and integrity. These are the life lessons that Mr. E gave me, lessons that I carry with me every day in business—the love and values that I call the Handshake Philosophy.

PART III

The Art of Real Estate Development

Something from Nothing

In the spring of my junior year of college, a band of friends and I got together to perform Mozart's *The Marriage of Figaro*. None of us was qualified to take on one of the true masterpieces of Western civilization. We were twenty years old. We were guided by a love of music and the joy of comedy, with a good dose of bravado, idealism, and sheer naïvety mixed in.

Each night we would move all the tables in the dining hall to one end. We built a stage and arranged the chairs in rows to create a makeshift theater. As the performance approached, volunteer musicians who comprised the orchestra would stream in with their instruments, handmade sets would rise, and colorful lights would be installed by volunteer carpenters and electricians. The performers changed into costumes of velvet and leather sewn by volunteer dressmakers and hatmakers. An audience of students filled the hall.

Performing a great opera was quite a challenge. I had to memorize three hours of music and dialogue. I had to act out situations I had yet to experience in life. But stepping out into the lights to wrestle with the work of one of the greatest geniuses in history was exhilarating. I still miss the camaraderie and excitement of those youthful performances.

The alchemy of these performances was that we made something from nothing. We took meager resources and a lot of energy and grit, and created something that was meaningful to others. We did not have majestic sets. No gilded carvings carried the audience to a mythical palace of the Count and Countess Almaviva in Seville. (The playwright Beaumarchais chose to set the story in exotic Spain so that its implicit social criticism would escape the watchful eyes of the French royal censors!) But with our willpower and artistic passion, we transported people. Perhaps they were daydreaming of their own childhoods, romances, or comic mishaps. Whether in comedy or tragedy, when opera reaches its audience, it allows the human spirit to soar.

Real estate development can aspire to a small taste of this spirit. You can take inspiration and grit and make something where there is nothing. The beauty of your work will impact how people feel in a space. Your vision of how people want to live or work will shape people's daily lives.

Within the constraints of law, you can situate your building at the top of a mountain or in a valley, facing south, north, east, or west, or more than one direction. You can choose the use of the building, from apartment to workplace to hotel. You can choose the shape and height of the building, the size and pattern of the windows, the color and texture of the materials, and the entrance experience. Given the same piece of land, no two developers would make the same building. This special power to impact the psychology and demand of your customer gives development a tremendous role to play in the story of real estate.

It was Christmas Eve 2010. We had just closed on 321 Ocean Drive in Miami Beach. It was exhilarating and daunting at the same time. People thought we were crazy to undertake such a project. Miami had been the epicenter of the condo bubble and subsequent crash. Down the street, a brand-new oceanfront property had just been seized by its lenders. But we realized we had something quite special—the last undeveloped oceanfront parcel of land in South Beach. We had found a great property at a great price. We knew people really wanted to be there. But to truly unlock the value of the site, we needed to build it!

321 Ocean sat directly on the sand, with spectacular views of

the ocean. We wanted to build something exquisite to match the natural beauty surrounding it. But the site had real challenges. It was a deep lot, 100 x 400 feet, sandwiched between two buildings. The way the zoning worked, you had to build a long, deep building that we nicknamed the "battleship." The site was great, but it needed a true transformation.

Creating something from nothing is the art of real estate development. You start with property that's not at its full potential, and you try to breathe life into it with limited resources. Our decision to produce an opera as students, undaunted by the greatness of the work and with innocent confidence, took hardly any physical or material resources. Yet it had a big impact. In real estate development, we also seek to create a meaningful experience for people, through architecture and floor plans. We also seek to make something from nothing. Our alchemy is taking earthen bricks, wood, and metal and shaping them into something that will serve and delight people.

When the lights dimmed and the orchestra tuned, the first notes of the overture could be heard. For three hours of *The Marriage of Figaro*, laughter erupted from the audience. Heartstrings were tugged. Mozart came to life.

As we walked by the empty lot that was 321 Ocean feeling the sea breeze, we wondered how we would live up to the beauty and rarity of the location. We faced the eternal question of development—how to take a bit of soil and inspiration and make something truly wonderful.

Investment and Development

Real estate development and investment can be two sides of the same coin. When you're investing, you want to buy things that cost less than they're worth. In real estate development, you work like crazy to make them worth more than they cost!

I'm a bit of an accidental developer. I earned my chops developing distressed assets and renovating old buildings. I'm not sure when it hit me that I might have found a calling in real estate development. Perhaps I had an inkling when we were grappling with the pneumatic caissons at William Street. It grew deeper tracking down the historic molds for The Bond canopy in Utah. Renovating The Alden, championing the tenants at The Clifton, and confronting the blank canvas of 321 Ocean were true catalysts for me.

At first, I figured development was just how you unlock the full value of your investment. I was trying to be a great investor. Little by little, I started to enjoy turning properties around and reimagining them. I discovered the fulfillment of another path on the journey from illiquidity to value, making something that serves and delights people.

Some legendary developers bet it all several times in a lifetime. Harry Macklowe already owned the General Motors Building on Fifth Avenue when he bought Sam Zell's office portfolio. He was forced to sell both to avoid collapse. He managed to hold on to another great New York site, the former Drake Hotel at 432 Park Avenue. During the downturn, I had looked at acquiring the mortgages secured by that land and deemed them too risky for the price. Some key pieces of the assemblage were still in the hands of foreign potentates and an elusive jeweler. Macklowe recapitalized the site and went on to build a modernist tower with soaring views of Central Park.

You don't have to take epic risks to develop real estate with the ethos of a value investor. You can decide which is cheaper, to buy or build. Buying an existing asset is a whole lot easier than building it yourself. But if the market is overpriced, overpaying for a "safe" cash-flowing asset may be riskier than building one for less.

Thoughtful development can also help you find value and manage risk. Something misunderstood can become beautiful and cash-flowing in the right hands. In development, you can mitigate risk by shaping your building with intimate knowledge of your customer. If you are a sharp-eyed student of human nature, neighborhoods, and culture, you can deliver something wonderful cheaply. Who is going to use the real estate you're making? How will they use it? Those are the key questions before embarking on a development.

That brings us to the fundamental principle of real estate development: know thy customer. Business is about serving people. Tech people use sophisticated tools and big data to understand consumer behavior in grand scale. We in real estate have to do it by hand, by foot, the old-fashioned way. It is a humanistic approach that I have distilled from my lifetime of curiosity around social philosophy, opera, and business. I strive to create buildings that deliver exactly what people want and need. If I can make it a meaningful experience for them without breaking the bank, I can create value through development.

Just as I've cultivated my own philosophy of investment in real estate, I develop real estate differently from anyone I know. I like to lavish love on every detail of the asset, the way in singing *bel canto* you lavish beauty on every note. My partner David and I spend countless hours obsessing over floor plans. We search for beautiful materials at a reasonable cost, inspired by the motto of Low Price with Meaning. We craft innovative rooms that respond to human needs. We have reconsidered what makes a great apartment in light of our philosophy. In Part III, I'd like to delve into the process I go through when developing real estate with my colleagues at Aria. I'd also like to share some observations about how real estate development fits within a larger conception of community.

While you don't have to embrace risk, you do need a lot of courage to be a developer. And you need to bring passion to your work. I learned a little bit of courage singing opera in front of a live audience, and passion by spending years to master a craft that can be a lifelong pursuit. Like investment, real estate development is something that you can work your whole life in and still continue to learn every day. I have come to love both disciplines.

Inspiration

Without inspiration, developments are cold, lifeless, and ugly. With it, real estate can charm, delight, and serve those who use it.

My father Carlos is a perfumer, a "nose" who creates the formulas for great fragrances. He finds inspiration in memories of his childhood in Tangier and Spanish Morocco, where he grew up in a loving, multigenerational family at the crossroads of several cultures. His scents are inspired by the violet and tobacco aromas of his grandfather's snuffbox, the mint tea that is lovingly poured with a dramatic flourish, and the laurel leaves and citrus fruit used in the Jewish festival of Sukkoth.

When my dad had to leave Morocco in 1967 and made his way through Paris, Amsterdam, Rio de Janeiro, and Buenos Aires, he found himself at an Argentine polo match. From the aromas of the grass, the horses, the earth, he conceived the fragrance Polo.

I start any new project by daydreaming and brainstorming on what the site could be. I had the good fortune to be born while my mom was getting her PhD in psychology, and her research was on creative play! Sometimes she would invite us kids to look at the clouds and find imaginary animals or faces.

I collect my ideas in an "inspiration book" filled with beautiful images and memories. The inspiration book for The Bond included canopies from around the world—grand hotels in London and Paris and the *beaux arts* jewels of Manhattan. I wanted to reimagine the run-down property as a grand building inspired by those of my childhood on the West Side.

I find history and life experiences can be fertile ground for inspiration in real estate. Sheep Meadow in Central Park was the site of many a Frisbee game when I was a teenager. It never crossed my mind that a flock of sheep once grazed there. What exactly were two hundred sheep doing in a public park in New York City?

Sheep Meadow was the brainchild of Frederick Law Olmsted and Calvert Vaux. The men who created Central Park believed that nature could have a powerful effect on people. They were inspired by the English garden, a wild, Romantic, man-made place that re-created nature in an idealized form. Carefully sculpted ponds and lakes were connected by bridges. Ruins of lost temples sat among groves of trees. It offered a way for Englishmen in the throes of urbanization and the industrial revolution to experience the calm and wonder of nature.

The great English Romantic poets of the nineteenth century conjured this landscape with the pen. In his 1818 poem "Endymion," Keats wrote, "A thing of beauty is a joy for ever. . . ." He exhorted his readers, tired from "over-darkened ways," to find meaning and solace in the landscape. And yes, Keats invoked sheep as part of the idealized landscape of his imagination!

Olmsted and Vaux practically invented landscape architecture to set this poetry into motion. They blasted it into the bedrock of New York using more gunpowder than the Battle of Gettysburg. They imported topsoil from New Jersey, deployed many species of trees and shrubs, and dug ponds and lakes to create a naturalistic effect. They wanted to provide a place where city dwellers could spiritually recharge.

Whereas the English garden was usually created for a nobleman to enjoy, Olmsted and Vaux wanted their park open to all. They believed that such a park was an important step for democracy. They rejected ornate gates in favor of more humble openings, to send the message that "all were welcome, regardless of rank or wealth." And they re-created a sheep meadow right out of the landscape of Romantic poetry as an antidote to the chaos of city life.

Nineteenth-century music was also enraptured by the Romantic landscape. After a master class in Vienna with a terrific Mexican tenor unexpectedly forced me to pick up a bit of German, I decided to learn and perform Beethoven's 1816 *An die ferne Geliebte*, or *To the Distant Beloved*. Some have hypothesized that the work was inspired by the composer's elusive "immortal beloved." The lyrics communicate directly with the Romantic landscape, asking for help. The singer pleads with the gurgling brooks, the rolling hills, the sunset over a lake, to convey his love across time and space. While I have a hard time getting through a newspaper in a German-speaking country, to this day I have no problem referring to nightingales and the last rays of the sun!

The landscape that captured my imagination as a child was my grandfather's house in Hartsdale, New York. An old fieldstone stair was flanked by ancient lilac trees, with fragrant but delicate purple and pink flowers. Climbing English roses covered the brickwork, and honeysuckle surrounded the columns. A massive oak tree provided shade for garden parties and backgammon games. For some unknown reason, a weathered stone bust of Queen Victoria was half-buried in a flower bed, like the ruins of the Romantic poets! It was a great place to let your mind wander.

Mr. E delighted in his gardens. In the summer, he would cut flowers and wrap the stems in wet paper towel and tin foil so we could take them home to the city. I came to love those gardens. As in the Beethoven song cycle, the landscape took on my feelings and emotions about this person who was so important in my life.

These memories came flooding back when I renovated The Bond apartments in Washington, DC. I thought English Romantic gardens at the entrance would be the perfect complement to reimagining the building with its new canopy. It's quite a challenge to create something with Romantic imagination, especially in the heart of the city. Working with a landscape architect who appreciated that style, we included topiary miniature roses, magnolia trees, Italian urns on pedestals filled with flowers, and even some half-buried stone sculptures! As a result, we created something beautiful and inviting for anyone who walks through.

We didn't include any sheep or lakes. We used the small space we were given. Henry David Thoreau it ain't. I love city living and I'm very comfortable in an urban environment. But we did evoke a feeling that only a Romantic garden can give—a calming respite from city bustle combined with a sense of creative adventure.

This process epitomized the joy of inspiration in real estate development. You get to share the experience of your most potent memories with others. You bring together landscape, architecture, light, and layouts to infuse a project with meaning. With memories of my grandfather's house as inspiration, we were able to give a small taste of Keats and a few bars of Beethoven to the residents of an apartment house in the heart of the city!

Land

Land is the vessel for the location of your project. You can change everything about the surface, you can build a hundred stories into the air, but you can't change the location, the land that it sits upon.

To develop a property, you have to think about what is special about that particular spot of earth. For Mr. E, the best land sat on a high point. Better air, cooler breeze. In the summers in Persia, he slept on the roof before air conditioning was invented. There was also a lower chance of being bitten by a scorpion! For Cousin Greg, location is about finding a piece of land at the right time in the cultural evolution of a great neighborhood.

I like to understand the overall meaning of the location to the person who's going to use it. The physical properties of the land— the hydrology, topography, sunlight, wind and hurricane corridors, seismic conditions, soil quality—represent the immutable place of your land in nature. Equally important is the place your land occupies in people's minds. How would they feel to be living or working there? Would they feel like they were a part of the action, or would it be an oasis away from the city? In a warm, authentic community, or off a dangerous highway at the end of the world? The answers to these questions form the basis for evaluating your land and deciding what to do with it. How to put your own stone in the edifice of man and nature.

My Yugoslavian chess coach Mr. Jovanovic used to invoke the Polish-Austro-Hungarian-Jewish-French chess grandmaster Savielly Tartakower, who famously stated that "Tactics is knowing what to do when there is something to do. Strategy is knowing what to do when there is nothing to do." In this interpretation, tactics is how you maneuver when there is an obvious move or initiative that calls out at you. Strategy is for times when you have to decide how to position yourself when there is no obvious move.

Much of real estate and value investment is tactics. It's about finding things that are mispriced and correcting misunderstandings. Finding a broken vase and putting it back together. Strategy can be dangerous in real estate. It may lead you to favor macro-generalizations that might prove wrong over microscopic anomalies that are easier to establish with certainty.

But strategy is essential when it comes to land. Land makes you consider what to do when there is nothing to do. You have infinite possibilities. Development requires an understanding of the competitive landscape, the highest and best use of the property, and whether this is the moment to pursue that particular use. Land, which most resembles an option to build in its deep financial structure, benefits greatly from the passage of time. Choosing when to exercise that option is especially tricky. If the neighborhood is improving, it's tempting to move quickly, but often waiting until the neighborhood ripens is the best bet.

At any moment you can pick up a shovel and add a new office building or hotel to the competitive marketplace. But you simultaneously give up the option to build an infinite number of alternative buildings or uses! You also give up the option to build the building in the future, when the best use may be more apparent or demand more solid. In prudent investment and development, you always have the option of doing nothing when there is nothing to do. Waiting to position yourself better before you attack can be a strategic triumph, whether on the chessboard or in real estate!

A great long-term strategy in land often calls for assemblage, where you stitch together multiple parcels to develop something significant. This can take years. Each city has its quirks of land use and zoning law that make assemblage a fascinating process. In places as diverse as the Netherlands, Vietnam, and Charleston, South Carolina, taxes were historically paid on frontage. Parcels there are skinny and deep. Other cities divided land into lots of 25 feet in width like New York, or 50 feet like Miami Beach. We have pursued developments that took several years of assemblage. We have one that may take decades! But the harder the assemblage is, the better the chance that you are finding value by assembling broken pieces.

I love to find things about a piece of land that other people don't see. In our block-through Boerum Hill development on my brother's laundromat in Brooklyn, most people saw Atlantic Avenue, a commercial thoroughfare. We saw Pacific Street with its brownstones and historic district. In our 1 Florida development, many saw the wrong side of NoMa, a brand-new first-class neighborhood to the south. I saw the right side of Bloomingdale, a beloved turn-of-the-century brownstone enclave with great places to go out. In a sense, it was reminiscent of what I saw in The Bond. A creative design process can often bring out the characteristics of several different neighborhoods on the same piece of land. You have to choose which to emphasize.

How you position your building on the land, both literally and figuratively, has a huge impact. This is one of the magical things you can do as a developer. In the early 2000s the Zeckendorf brothers, heirs to a legendary New York development dynasty, bought the old Mayflower Hotel site on the West Side, an entire block spanning from Central Park West to Broadway. When we were working on William Street, we had looked at acquiring the site, but it seemed too expensive and complex. While the majority of the buildable density was situated on Broadway, it was fraught with landmark considerations because it was visible from Central Park. It almost seemed like two sites—one historically protected site on Central

REAL ESTATE, A LOVE STORY

Park West and another on Broadway where most of the density would go. The price didn't seem justified because only a small part of the building was truly on Central Park West.

The Zeckendorfs hired Robert Stern, a Yale professor of historically inspired architecture, to set the tone in keeping with the other grand Central Park West buildings. They created a twelve-story building on Central Park West, and a much taller tower on Broadway. But they made a critical decision that sealed the success of the project—both buildings used the same entrance right across from the park, and the Central Park West address became the name of the building! The architecture ensured a Central Park West glow, even for the majority of the units physically located above Broadway. The apartments were incredibly well received and sold for a fortune. Essentially, they had bought land on Broadway and sold Central Park West, capturing an arbitrage in meaning.

Architecture

Architecture is the language in which you express your inspiration and business plan. It allows you to affect people's mood while carrying out essential functions, just as the words you use each day convey literal meaning but also make people feel a certain way.

We wanted to find an inspiring architect for 321 Ocean, one who could live up to the site's natural beauty, and make it a place where people really wanted to be. We also needed an architect to help share our vision with the community and build support for the project. We met with several architects to listen and learn.

Richard Meier brought his soulful blue eyes and turquoise bracelet to the table, as well as a vision of beauty for the project. He emanated a kind of spiritual energy. Meier had done a pair of stunning oceanfront buildings in Jesolo, Italy, that formed part of our inspiration for the project. His white aesthetic seemed perfect for Miami and its spectacular blinding light (one smart aleck called his white New York buildings Miami on the Hudson!).

We felt big balconies were essential to creating a great residential building in Miami. While most people hardly ever use balconies, they love to have them. But most of the time balconies make a building look ugly. Meier's buildings had gorgeous balconies. Yet we feared the cost implications of going with such a glass-oriented architect. We were also concerned that in choosing to work with such a renowned figure, we might not be able to make changes that are often necessary for the economics of a project. We were coming out of the Great Recession and had not forgotten value investment! We absolutely needed to make the project a success by keeping the costs reasonable.

Next, we met with Enrique Norten, an important Mexican architect. He appreciated the character of the site and its urban infill context, having created many similar buildings in Mexico City and New York. His buildings were not isolated towers. They formed part of the fabric of the city. Norten brought a pure modernism, but a modernism tempered by the tropical climate of his native land. He also brought a "roll up your sleeves" attitude to the project. He seemed willing to work with us to ensure the project would be a success. It was a thoughtful and reasonable approach. Norten never wavered in his architectural principles, but he always found a way to make them work with the needs of the future residents and the project.

We wanted to explore another architectural style, so we met with Rafael Viñoly, a highly regarded Uruguayan architect. He had done urban projects as well as soaring towers. We wondered if he could help make our project soar, given its proximity to nature and the ocean, despite its urban infill location. Viñoly had an irrepressible creative energy and wielded a black pen with panache.

Viñoly made a grand entrance with a Japanese colleague and greeted us warmly. After that he was continuously interrupted by calls on his cell phone. We presented him with our challenge—getting as much of the project to have a view of the ocean as possible. He had done a beautiful pyramidal building in Uruguay that we loved. But we thought the solution was not applicable to our site because of the immediate context.

Pen in hand and cell phone on ear, he drew a section of a pyramidal structure where the units were stacked diagonally. Each was offset backward by a half floor, so that instead of seven stories we had fourteen overlapping half stories. He proved that he was correct. You could in fact give every unit an ocean view! And he also proved that he wasn't terribly interested in a practical approach or working collaboratively. It was tempting, but ultimately a no-go. We decided to work with Enrique.

It was no big loss for Viñoly. We finally realized why he was so distracted. As we were leaving, we bumped into Harry Macklowe, who was about to hire him for the ninety-six-story 432 Park Avenue, the tallest residential structure in the Western Hemisphere!

Modernism

Truth be told, I was a bit nervous about committing to modern architecture for our work at 321 Ocean. Having grown up inspired by historic beauty, I wasn't sure about modernism. But working with Enrique taught me a lot about architecture. I came to admire his commitment to his craft, and his results won me over.

The first modernist painting is arguably Picasso's *Girl with a Mandolin*. It breaks things down to their constituent parts, revealing their underlying structure. Instead of finding beauty in the whole, cubism reveals the deeper structure of the parts, as Cézanne had done with cones, spheres, and cubes (and Tufano's method had done with bonds and options!). As I learned from Enrique, it's the same in modern buildings. The deeper truth of form is function and structure, and modern buildings are often raw forms, volumes in space like Picasso's portrait.

Enrique's architecture felt like cubism in three dimensions. He conceived of the building's mass as distinct volumes, much like Picasso's *Girl with a Mandolin*. Enrique had one cardinal rule in his creation and juxtaposition of volumes—that the same plane couldn't have two materials. Structural volumes have integrity and honesty. That must be revealed transparently such that each volume is made of one material. To Enrique, changing materials on the same volume is vulgar and dishonest. In Keats, Truth is Beauty. In modern art, Beauty is Truth.

There is beauty in simplicity. Minimalism can have a meaning and beauty of its own. Some of the best modernist works wed pure forms to beautiful materials, or they interact with light to give a building a more beautiful expression of the whole. It is said that in painting, the form carries the rational and intellectual message, where the color carries the emotional content. In architecture, the form and volumes appeal to the rational mind, and the materials appeal to the emotions.

Modernism with natural materials and light informed tropical modernism, the school of South American architects who adapted modernism to local conditions with wood, stone, and lush greenery. Their modernism is softer and more organic, and it can be very beautiful because it joins with nature. For me, tropical modernism is a little like listening to Plàcido Domingo sing *Die Walküre*!

But modern art often wants us to see the world as only truth, to hold a mirror up to the world. That's fine for philosophers. But for art and music and architecture, there is often a contention that the truth is really that the world is ugly and horrible, society is corrupt and unjust and irredeemable. The mirror held up to the viewer is broken and fragmented.

The great luminaries of literature—Shakespeare, Tolstoy—didn't think of life as something purely evil and broken that had to be denounced and unveiled. They envisioned the whole of life as a tapestry of beauty. I don't believe that there is more truth in ugliness than there is in beauty. It makes you sound smart. It makes you sound like a profound thinker pulling the wool off our eyes. But deep down I don't believe it.

Nowhere is an extreme modernist approach more alarming than in modern opera productions. Starting in Europe, where state subsidies allow the audience to be ignored, and increasingly in America, opera has been the subject of vulgar, supposedly modern productions that desecrate some of the greatest works of art. They set the opera in Las Vegas, or on a toilet, or in some politically expedient other era. They disassemble the work of art, which was a coherent act of music and words that have meaning, and in fragmenting the work they often render the words meaningless. This to me is a terrible sin, because it undermines the fundamental principle of operatic expression, *dramma per musica*, that the words and the music go together.

It's often said that this is necessary to attract a younger audience, who want to see more innovative interpretations. I say this is malarkey. They never have the chance to fall in love with the opera itself, the work of art as the composer intended it. Many of these operas have survived for two hundred years. It's not because of vulgar interpretations seeking to tell the truth about patriarchy, ugliness, or the political failings of our society. They have survived because they are beautiful and speak to timeless facets of the human condition. No one has ever fallen in love with opera through a modern opera production. You can't fall in love with a self-critical cold fish.

Modernism at its worst prizes function over form, and elevates the parts over the whole. The Pompidou Centre in Paris, with its stark truth-telling and inside-out functionality, projects a strong commitment to truth over beauty or goodness or soulfulness. It is so concerned with telling the truth about the structure, what's honestly holding it up, the pipes, the air conditioning, that it forgets what makes it a great building. Architecture was founded to elevate the spirit. Modernism, in its effort to be truthful and honest about the parts, neglects the feelings the whole exerts on the viewer or user. Modernism can be powerful when it mixes truth with beauty, and reason with emotion. Without both elements, modernism lacks humanity.

Great architects make development more beautiful and exciting. But if you have a strong inspiration and vision for the site, you have to work hand in hand to realize that vision. If you are speaking one language and your architect is speaking another, you may end up with your very own Tower of Babel!

Light

You can imagine my surprise when I discovered that Enrique had designed a metallic louver system to cover part of the western facade of 321 Ocean. This was a building we designed for delight. That side held the more modest units that we as the developers hoped to buy and enjoy in the future. Now an industrial metal sheath was going to shield the front of the building—including my prospective living room! I wanted to spend time in Miami because of the sun. I had spent my whole life in New York surrounded by concrete and metal. The last thing I wanted was a coat of chain mail to cover my sunsets. I was incensed.

Enrique argued strongly for the louver system as an integral part of the architectural design. Out of respect, we gave him the benefit of the doubt. His point was that the sun in tropical climates can be hell. If you face west, you want some sun protection in the afternoon. It turns out he had even designed his own house in Mexico City replete with louvers for shade. I swallowed my pride and went along with it for the good of the project.

When the building was unveiled, I was devastated. The entire west side of my living room was louvered in metal. I was outraged. Worse yet, my wife was outraged! Why had we left New York for this? What moron had allowed the architect to do this? It would render the place uninhabitable, and there was no one else to blame. I figured we had to come up with a solution to make the louvers disappear. We ordered sheer linen curtains to ring the perimeter of the living room. At least with that flourish, the windows appeared continuous and harmonious, notwithstanding the hulking metal that lay just across the glass.

Little by little, as we began to inhabit the space, strange things started happening. At sunset, a beautiful latticework of shadow was cast across the walls in diagonals. It would walk across the room as the sun sank in the sky. The geometry of the facade was projected across the living room like a sundial. There was no shortage of light, and it actually gave us a more vivid experience of sunset than without the louvers. At last Enrique's vision had come true. Now I wouldn't let go of those louvers for anything.

How architects shape and bend light to enrich the human experience is one of the great mysteries of real estate. It begins with the spiritual purpose of the original architects—Stonehenge, the Acropolis, the Temple of Solomon. Each offers a different model of light in architecture. All architecture in a sense mediates between man and nature, between man and God. Architecture is about connecting human beings to the sacred. And real estate development can be too. It's a tiny bit of creation, in the same way that traditional Judaism views circumcision as letting man complete the act of creation. Only hopefully not as painful.

Spirit

There is a beautiful chapel on the campus of Harvard Business School designed by the architect Moshe Safdie. One of its principal virtues is how it brings light into the space. Imagine a copper cylinder that intersects a glass pyramid. As if a reflection, a Japanese garden is sunk into the ground in an inverted pyramid. Inside the cylinder is entirely pale concrete. Prisms in a skylight cast rainbows across the spartan concrete walls in ever-changing shapes that morph with the trajectory of the sun and the passage of clouds. The quality of light evokes a feeling of sacredness. I used to love to sneak out of my rigorous business school schedule and sit quietly in the space. I'm not sure why I was usually the only one there. More than likely, I was one of the handful of introverts among the thousand extroverts in each class.

The prisms of the HBS chapel project a spiritual light that changes form and color as the sun moves across the sky. This gives you a special experience of the sun and the passage of time much like Enrique's louvers. Prisms bend light and give you light's dazzle and color. They remind me of the Bohemian crystal prisms that comprised Mr. E's chandeliers, where a ray of light can create fire and divinity.

The stained glass of Sainte Chapelle in Paris filters light and softens it. It is echoed in churches and synagogues around the world. Medieval architecture relied on heavy bearing walls that allowed in much less light. In these buildings, often in northern climates, the color of the stained glass creates a spiritual glow in the room. The sun is rarer, and oblique shafts of light come in through the front door or through the colored glass, representing the divine spirit.

These are prayerful, soulful rooms that make use of just a little light. With glass and color, they magnify its primal power.

It occurred to me that perhaps this is why the magic of cinema does so much to transport moviegoers. You are in a dark room, with light projected obliquely through the equivalent of stained glass—film. You hear music, words, and deep emotion. Perhaps this is part of why movies are a spiritual experience for so many people.

There are three archetypal light forms that inform all of architecture—sunlight, fire, and moonlight. Architects craft buildings to bask in these different forms of light. Light has a lot to do with the experience you have when you're in those spaces. To develop great real estate, you have to keep that in mind.

Sunlight strongly informed our development at 321 Ocean, and not just with the louvers. With a tight site, we worked relentlessly on the floor plans to make sure every unit enjoyed beautiful sunlight. To accomplish this, we crafted floor-though units running east-west. In the same apartment, you can wake up with the sunrise in your bedroom, and have a drink or unwind with the family at sunset.

Firelight emits a totally different kind of energy than sunlight. Humans have been using fire for 800,000 years. It recalls our days as humans around a campfire that provided light and warmth and cooked our food. It's a cozier, more intimate light. It projects upward on human faces and comforts us.

In nineteenth-century opera, the stage was lit by a small fire that was reflected up into the faces of the performers with lime. The uplighting created a drama of light and shadow on the actors' faces. But the light reflected by the lime didn't go very far, so the actors had to step forward to catch the light. When artists seek the "limelight," they are stepping into that primal firelight.

I remember being struck by a certain light quality in the Mercer

Hotel in SoHo. The exposed brick walls are lit from below and grazed by the light coming upward. The texture of the brick wall creates shadows and relief. Uplighting creates a simultaneously intimate and dramatic effect. When you need a dramatic room, uplighting can provide the answer. Perhaps this is the power of firelight. It comes from below and projects light and shadows onto human faces, the ultimate bas-relief.

Moonlight conjures another energy. It is the light of poets, from Shakespeare's *Romeo and Juliet* to *Rusalka* with its song to the silvery moon. Because moonlight is sunlight reflected off the moon's surface, it has a cooler tone and a silvery quality that adds to its mystery. This is harder to capture in real estate, unless you sleep on the roof, as my grandfather did! But we have been able to give people Juliet balconies in some projects, where you can enjoy the romance of the stars from inside your apartment. Or you can appreciate moonlight on a roof deck that we are incorporating into all our new buildings!

Sitting in the Moshe Sadie chapel at HBS, I watched the sun slowly traverse the sky. Light refracted in brilliant color on the concrete walls. This was the perfect place for quiet contemplation amidst the excitement of business. It was a quiet reminder that the original purpose of real estate was to infuse human life with a little bit of the sacred.

Community

One day in 1958, Frank Del Vecchio was flying himself home from the *USS Franklin D. Roosevelt*, where he was stationed with the United States Navy. Frank was a "hot cat pilot," which meant he waited in his McDonnell F3H-2N Demon fighter plane rain or shine attached to a steam catapult. He was ready to be launched off the aircraft carrier on a moment's notice at the appearance of enemy aircraft.

Frank had grown up in the West End of Boston, an immigrant neighborhood where the aromas of Italian cooking mingled with the strains of the Jewish cantors singing Sabbath prayers. Frank's family told him that their entire neighborhood in Boston was being demolished in the name of urban renewal. Frank decided to go see for himself and found the street where he had grown up. When he looked up, he could see the wallpaper of his childhood bedroom in the half-demolished apartment house.

Frank decided to fight to make sure that this kind of neighborhood demolition wouldn't happen again. He enrolled in Harvard Law School and met a Radcliffe student named Marian, who became his partner in crime. They went to Washington, DC, to help roll out a community-based housing program. It was led by the pastors of prominent local churches, and none other than Martin Luther King Jr.

Frank's organization promised to help revitalize neighborhoods without destroying them. They had just hit their stride when Dr. King was assassinated. Large parts of the neighborhood burned to the ground in the riots that followed. Frank was disillusioned. But he devoted his career to championing housing and fairness at the US Department of Housing and Urban Development for many years. After he retired, Frank discovered a second career in Miami Beach as a prominent civic activist. He became a guardian of neighborhoods and championed the cause of justice in municipal government.

Of course, we didn't know any of this when David, Tim, and I went to meet Frank for coffee. Little did we know that Frank Del Vecchio would teach us a lot about development, community, and idealism.

By total coincidence, Frank lived next door to our project. He was kind of the unofficial mayor of the South of Fifth neighborhood. We stepped into the meeting unsure of what to expect. We found a fighter pilot who, in his own words, "carried an atomic bomb in his pocket." He also carried a typed list of the things that were absolutely not permitted on the site. They were the Ten Commandments of developing in his neighborhood!

At the top of Frank's list of no-no's was building a hotel with a loud restaurant, one that in his experience would inevitably become a nightclub in the heart of a residential neighborhood. That wasn't our modus operandi, but Frank had seen a lot of developers come and go in his years in Miami Beach. Few of them were true to their word. I remember Frank saying he would keep an open mind but warned emphatically he would "break with us" if we went back on our word!

Over time, we got to know Frank and his story. We came to understand why he approached neighborhoods and democracy with such purpose. He described Miami Beach politics as a vibrant "Athenian democracy" where everyone gets a voice. So we took our ideas on the road. We met with dozens of civic groups and local leaders, neighbors, historic preservationists, and noise pollution activists. We wanted to understand what the neighborhood wanted, and if that could work economically and architecturally for the project. Frank and other civic leaders continually challenged us to do better, to forge a solution hand in hand with our neighbors.

The outlines of a win-win compromise with the neighborhood began to emerge. We would do a purely residential building on the site. No hotel, no short-term rentals, no restaurant, no bar whatsoever. That would be inscribed on the deed of the property in perpetuity. We would double the side setbacks and create a courtyard in the middle of the site. That would let a lot more light and air in for the neighbors. Our request was to take the footage we would shave off the sides and carve from the courtyard and put it on top of the oceanfront building. This would require twenty-five feet in additional height.

We went to an art supply store and bought some balsa wood and glue. We built a rough scale model of the "battleship" building allowed by right under current zoning, and another of the courtyard-centered building with a lot more light and air.

Any zoning change would apply not just to our site but to any comparable site in the Ocean Beach Historic District. We believed such a change would be helpful to the neighborhood in creating a more harmonious urban design. For fear of corruption, or silver-tongued developers talking their way into more height, Miami Beach had changed the zoning ordinance to limit development. They made it so that no one could get a variance for height, a routine process usually driven by city planning staff. Changing height in a Miami Beach neighborhood required an act of the City Commission!

It was a year's work with no guarantee of success. Inspired by the balsa wood model and how much better it seemed for the neighborhood and the project, we decided to give it a try. After much back-and-forth, both neighboring condominium associations agreed to support the proposal. Other neighborhood groups signed on. To build more public support for the project, we held a forum at the Miami Design Preservation League, which was well received. We formed a coalition with neighborhood groups that would take the proposed bill to the Historic Preservation Board, and if we could succeed there, to the City Commission.

Enrique Norten led our presentation before the Historic Preservation Board. With his candor and respect, he pointed out that the current zoning would be "perfect for a Holiday Inn," but not for a beautiful residential building. His analysis of the urban design context illustrated a startling observation—virtually all of the nearby buildings along the water had exactly the same height we were proposing. A small zoning change to improve the neighborhood and the project would be, in Enrique's endearing Mexican accent, "How do you say in your country, a no-brainer." We received the recommendation of the Historic Preservation Board and proceeded to the City Commission.

The City Commission was a more political forum. Frank, who was unbelievably talented in civic law, knew all of the council members well, and his reputation for integrity was unassailable. The mayor, however, opposed the bill. "If you want to play cards with me, I can play cards with you." At the first reading of the bill, she was absent, and the bill passed 6–0. At the second reading, it was 6–1. But we had won by the supermajority needed. The bill passed! And the opportunity to forge a coalition with the neighborhood was saved.

It was an incredible lesson in real estate as a branch of civics. Frank's Ten Commandments became a touchstone of our work, a standard to aspire to throughout our careers. We learned that building a neighborhood coalition is a critical part of real estate development. Respecting people and hearing every voice can make the project better for everyone. With his incredibly high standards and idealism, Frank Del Vecchio had shown us to develop with a larger purpose.

Real Estate Humanism

There's an incredible scene in the documentary *Chef's Table* when the filmmaker interviews Dan Barber, one of the pioneers of the farm-to-table movement in America. These guys have radically changed the supply chain and how food gets to restaurants in major cities in the country. In 2016, restaurants eclipsed home cooking in dollars spent on food for the first time in history. The documentary is beautifully produced and got me completely hooked on two things that I usually avoid—fine cuisine and television. But what really animates the show are the life stories of the chefs, whose biographies are the centerpiece of each episode.

The episode shows Dan Barber meeting an agronomist at Cornell who has spent his whole life breeding plants. Barber implores him to give him a squash with a deep, rich flavor and without the extra wateriness and size. The agronomist is dumbfounded. Everyone has asked him to breed for yield. For durability. No one has ever asked him to breed for taste. And that's the trouble with real estate today. People are building for profit or to code, not for taste. No one asks the mason or even the architect to build for taste, or smell, or delight. Just as there's a niche in the food world for breeding for taste, there's an underserved niche in real estate development for building for delight.

I believe in a human-centered real estate. Humanism has to permeate both the buildings that you build and the way that you interact with the people in the process. A couple of hundred people have their hands in the creation of a building. Each has a different goal. The mason wants to put down bricks. The scaffold guy wants to install scaffolding. The architect wants the place to look good.

The city wants the permit in order. The lender wants to be repaid. It's left to the developer to remember that the goal is a wonderful building at a reasonable price—for people.

The golden age for this way of thinking was the Renaissance. Beauty in art and architecture was centered on the human form. Leonardo da Vinci tried to distill the principles of design and beauty from the human figure, so as to invent new ways to delight people. He went back to the ancient Roman architect Vitruvius, who believed in both form and function. Vitruvius thought that there were deep relationships embodied in the human form that govern shape and proportion—the Golden Ratio. This ideal ratio would hold true for rooms in buildings or the shape of canvases for painting (a present-day equivalent would be aspect ratios—the differing proportions of screens for films, televisions, computers, and social media posts!).

According to da Vinci, the Golden Ratio is to be found in the human form. His famous illustration of the Vitruvian Man inside a circle illustrates his view that humanity exhibits divine perfection, and design must reflect that. Humanism was the common thread in his work.

Inspired real estate development must drink from the same fountain as da Vinci. Keeping your human orientation in the real estate business is how you stay grounded and is also part of finding business success. Because if you are designing for humans, or designing for taste, as in the *Chef's Table* documentary, you are assured a warm and likely profitable reception for your product.

There are two ways to do this. The first is to connect to people on a basic level with empathy in your daily interactions. You can be down-to-earth and humane and have some generosity of spirit in your business dealings. Give people the benefit of the doubt and see if they treat you well too. Usually they do. And if they don't, they'd better look out! This is what I have called the Handshake Philosophy.

The second way to humanize your business is to think about your customer as a person. It's a lot harder than it sounds. You have to deliver a myriad of technical details and mind the bottom line. But satisfaction and success ultimately come if you discover how to delight the customer. Humanistic development requires empathy and understanding. A great example of this comes from the architects for an assisted-living project who had a creative idea. They spent the day blindfolded to understand how a vision-impaired person might feel navigating the space!

My favorite example of humanistic design comes from outside real estate. Apple humanized the computer. Steve Jobs embraced what real estate people call placemaking: making a familiar environment in which to think. Instead of the ones and zeroes of code, he gave people a desktop with familiar objects from the real world, like folders and trash. Architecture in the service of meaning impacts how people feel when they're in a space. Jobs did this for computers, making them a place where humans are welcome and can relate.

Fortunately for us, Steve Jobs fell in love with calligraphy and incorporated beauty into his operating system. In what had hitherto been a mechanistic world of dull green light, Jobs allowed people to imitate handwriting and chose different aesthetics. He added an element of human expression to what had been merely word processing and allowed people to tap into their creativity.

Jobs reinvented Apple several times, each time with a humanistic vision. He revived Macintosh with colorful computers and a simple, minimalist beauty. He created the iPod so people could easily listen to music. And he created the iPhone, which brought beauty and color and life to a telephone. Imagine how much joy he brought to countless people. His products are so human, they're too addictive!

This is how we aspire to develop, to build real estate: with a humanistic vision and an understanding of what delights and brings meaning to people. In my career, I've tried to capture both sides of a humanistic outlook: on a person-to-person level, and in creating a humanistic product that seeks to make people happy. The moments where I've felt most excited as a developer were those where I found a way to live up to this humanistic goal—building someone a home, reimagining how people inhabit a space, working with a community, or participating in the rebirth of a neighborhood.

Transformation

You can look at a hunk of stone in many different ways. Some see gravel. Others see a wall. Michelangelo looked at a two-ton hunk of rough-hewn marble and saw a magnificent sculpture in human form.

Transformation is the sister of inspiration. When you look at a building or a plot of land, you have to envision the potential for transformation. If you have an inspired vision for how things could be, you have to make it so.

Experience shows that transformation through development is real. I saw a defunct elevated railroad in Manhattan become the High Line. I witnessed the Prison Bus drop-off in Long Island City become a vibrant neighborhood. I nursed The Alden back to health, from a bullet-riddled shell to happily occupied mixed-income apartments. Together these experiences gave me faith in the developer's ability to reimagine a property.

So I listened closely when I was approached about buying a massive, 400,000-square-foot 1960s office building outside DC. The ten-story building was about to be completely empty and was burning through cash. In 2006, at the top of the market, the owners had taken out a $43.5 million loan with Countrywide, a poster child of the housing bubble. Now the property was in foreclosure and could be bought for pennies on the dollar, less than $25 per foot. It was a deep value play and a project that needed reimagining.

Anoop Davé, my colleague at Square Mile Capital as the wheels came off in the last cycle, found the deal. I remember taking the train from Greenwich to New York with Anoop one day in 2007. We perused the prospectus for a loan to a land developer at the peak of the housing bubble. It was being marketed by Lehman Brothers. One of the deal highlights was that the company was putting in fresh equity of some $250 million. As a lender, it's usually a good sign if the owners are eating their own cooking. If you looked really closely, though, they were simultaneously pulling out some $2 billion from the loan proceeds! The sponsors were getting out while the getting was good. Anoop shares my love of a bargain, and shock at a blatant misrepresentation. We were both astounded. It felt like one of the signs of the apocalypse, which in a sense it was. After that, when Anoop liked a deal, it meant a lot.

The deal was located in Hyattsville, Maryland, just outside the DC boundary, a short walk from the DC Metro's Green Line. It was a master-planned neighborhood not far from the University of Maryland. Anoop was working in Washington with the Bernstein Companies, a well-reputed DC player that had just made a deal to build the new Marriott headquarters in Bethesda. Anoop had found this deep value situation because the Bernsteins owned other property in the neighborhood. Hyattsville had emerged as an arts community in recent years, with studios and galleries popping up amidst cool coffee shops and old-time stores with a lot of character.

But this property was a white elephant. It was the same size as the Lenox China factory, 400,000 square feet of empty. The office market in suburban DC, even with the Metro, was a disaster. But we had an idea up our sleeve. What if we took this gigantic office building that no one wanted and turned it into an apartment building? It turns out a couple of major REITs had apartment buildings in the immediate vicinity. They were 97 percent leased.

The building was a monumental 1960s edifice designed by Edward Durrell Stone, an architect famous for the Kennedy Center in DC. It had gigantic floor plates suitable for hundreds of employees but too large for traditional apartment design. Tens of thousands of feet would be wasted, making the project uneconomical. Furthermore, the building had been designed with bay windows on a ten-foot grid, each shaped like the cockpit of a supersonic airplane. They provided a ton of light into the building at all angles. But while the design probably felt futuristic in 1960s, it was disorienting today. We needed a creative floor plan strategy to reimagine the building as apartments.

My uncles had a strategy for converting high-ceilinged office buildings with deep floor plates into apartments. They put a sleeping loft over the kitchen. In a sense, they rotated the apartments ninety degrees vertically to get more usage out of the same space. But when we took the measurements, the Hyattsville building didn't quite have the height to make this viable.

Anoop had an ace in the hole. Years before, he had converted a bunch of office buildings with his former boss Ron Caplan. Ron is tough as nails and a construction genius. He had converted thousands of apartments in Center City Philadelphia. Ron had discovered that units could be rotated ninety degrees horizontally in very deep spaces. Instead of having a typical bedroom next to the living room on the perimeter of the building, you could peel the bedroom off the windows and put it inboard of the living room. It was based on the premise that people don't need a big window while they sleep anyway, but they love a huge living room. You could even make a sliding door or French door to let light into the bedroom.

We decided to do some research to see if this might work in the Hyattsville project. We soon discovered that the rotated layout was so efficient in deep spaces that some very big players had started using them—not just to convert offices, but on new buildings as well! After a lot of study and some regression analysis, we found that there wasn't a big price discount for having the inboard bedrooms. By rotating the traditional design, we were able to give almost all the apartments two bay windows. Each would get a twenty-foot living room and tons of light!

Renovation is a great discipline in which to learn development. It forces you to squeeze every drop from every square inch of real estate. The exterior box is fixed, so floor plans become the essential variable in determining your outcome. That discipline is highly applicable to ground-up development. You generally have only a finite number of square feet that you can build. You try to squeeze value out of every inch. When you make every square foot useful to people, you also maximize the potential rent per foot.

In our Hyattsville renovation, a creative approach to the floor plans enabled us to transform the project from office to residential. With a little inspiration and floor plan magic, we were able to reimagine an illiquid, empty office building as an innovative and efficient apartment house for a vibrant artistic community. When it opens, we will know if the transformation is complete!

Frozen Music

If architecture is "frozen music," as Goethe famously observed, then floor plans are frozen business plans. They are the silent force that organizes movement around a space. Like the one hundred most common words with Old English roots, they are largely unseen. They are literally hidden beneath your feet. Floor plan decisions are huge and too important to leave solely to the architects. They are your business plan in architectural form.

Real estate investors and developers are often focused on square feet as a metric to judge an apartment. But people don't live in square feet. They experience a space. How it looks and how it feels. As my partner David Arditi likes to say, "Not all square feet are created equal." Finding the right square feet to emphasize, while eliminating those that are not useful, lets you deliver a lot more bang for the buck.

Small and efficient floor plans done right can create value for your tenants. For a low dollar price, they can enjoy the same functionality and delight they would in a larger apartment. This unites development with value investment. If your goal is to deliver value with meaning to the customer, doing so in a smaller package at a lower cost mitigates your risk.

Renovation taught me to develop real estate with efficient small units and lots of bedrooms, true to my value instincts. I am seeking soulful minimalism that is cheap but good. It brings together the Low Price with Meaning of the IKEA case and my minimalist rooms at Domus Pacis in Rome, with my uncles' floor plans and the frugality of Mr. E. I cut my teeth in renovation of The Alden and The Bond, adapting New York tenement buildings with my uncles' advice. This is how we came to love smaller units and shared apartments.

Imagine the tenants as a miniature army of real estate value investors. They are trying to get the most bang for the buck too. Development allows you to put yourself in their shoes. As a value investor, you put in dollars mixed with brainpower, structure, and patience, and get out cash flows. A person or a company pays rent and gets ostensibly space, but also, more deeply, an experience. The developer who really understands the end user can create value as an investor. After all, people are the protagonists of their own story, living their lives. You have to give them function and meaning. If you can shape space to give them joy in their work or life, your project will be a success.

Throughout life there are expensive ways to be happy and inexpensive ones. As a kid I spent countless hours playing Ping-Pong with Mr. E on the homemade table he and his brothers were so proud of. It lasted a good thirty years and was made of simple plywood and plumbing pipes.

Sometimes a small gesture can make a large impact. A few months ago, my youngest son made a gesture that surprised and touched me. He offered his blanket to his big brother. As a toddler, his blanket is his favorite object. He cuddles with it, he sniffs it, he luxuriates in it. When he offered it to his brother, it was a small gesture of love that hit the mark!

When I develop today, I try to find the most simple and affordable ways to make people happy and have an impact. I like to consider this a kind of soulful minimalism. It means highlighting only the most essential aspects of a product or experience to reduce the cost, and then layering on the most delightful and joyful aspects of that same product or experience.

In business, you aren't given infinite resources to please your customer. You have to learn how to make them happy with just a few small gestures. And to discover this, the best way is to try it yourself. Can you satisfy your needs frugally with a small apartment, solo or shared, as I had at Domus Pacis? Many millennials in the wake of the Great Recession are discovering that they prefer to derive meaning in life from experiences and work rather than stuff. And we are reimagining apartment design to suit them with gestures grand and small.

Reimagining the Apartment

We recently did a project with a group of HBS students to understand how the millennial generation sees housing. The results were eye-opening and exciting. You'll never guess what their biggest concern was! I expected to hear the usual ones about apartments, the size, location, kitchen, closets—the things apartment developers usually focus on. Think for a moment what might be the most salient concern of the next generation of apartment residents.

The most pressing issue for the millennial cohort in our study was package delivery! Doormen in New York used to be there for an extra layer of security. I had a doorman who had stashed a baseball bat just in case. Now they have been transformed into longshoremen, presiding over an ever-increasing influx of packages! As a developer, we need to accommodate this change in the way people live.

More broadly, we observed that the younger tenants saw real estate more as an experience than as a product or asset class. They wanted to feel honesty and transparency, and they wanted to live frugally. They wanted to pay less for rent but still have a great experience. It sounded a lot like Low Cost with Meaning. This mindset resonated with what we were doing in our DC projects and what my uncles had done in New York. So we have taken all our learnings from millennial-oriented apartment successes and applied them to new projects.

It's an approach to real estate that I call soulful minimalism. How to deliver an apartment at a lower price with meaning, so people can afford to live in great cities and also feel good in their home. This became my source of inspiration in trying to reinvent apartments for the next generation of residents. In each project, we have tried to produce a slightly better apartment.

Here's a fantasy to show you how the creative process works. I'm thinking out loud. This is how I approach any new project. Many of the ideas are foolish. But if there's one good idea in there, it will have been worth it.

Let's exercise our poetic faith, what Coleridge called our "willing suspension of disbelief." I could never develop real estate (or love opera!) if I couldn't voluntarily suspend my skepticism to imagine what is possible. It's very easy to use your rational faculties and shoot down ideas. It's much harder to do business from a place of joy and inspiration. How would you create your frugal fantasy apartment? Come with me on this experiment and then try it if you enjoy it.

When did you last find joy in a smaller space? Going back through memories can help distill the essence of what makes an experience meaningful. For me, a flood of positive experiences in places comes rushing back. From Domus Pacis to my compact apartment in New York to a hut in the foothills of the Himalayas.

A great apartment delivers the essentials in a wonderful way. It has to be a place to find your zen and recharge before facing the world another time. A great place to take a shower, pour yourself a glass of wine, have a date over, hang out with a friend, or crash. To make coffee or tea and keep warm in the winter. My ideal apartment is close to public transportation, or ideally within walking distance to work. The road rage is gone, and it means more time with the kids.

To make it affordable, the apartment can't be a palace. If we lived in a world where everyone had a private jet and a 5,000-square-foot apartment, development would be simple. It is fairly easy to spend infinite resources to create the most luxurious apartment possible.

It's much more exciting and challenging to create a wonderful apartment with less. It's basically the business application of economics to property development—how to flourish in a world of scarce resources. Yet while there are scarce material resources, the human imagination is unlimited.

We have to deliver life's essentials in a smaller package. So let's make things a little more challenging. Let's assume that the apartment is only 400 square feet!

What kind of a kitchen would this unit have? In New York I have tons of friends who use their oven for extra storage since space is so tight. OK, maybe that's actually me. What about a kitchen with just the essentials that bring people joy? A great espresso maker. A wine fridge. A blender to make smoothies. In my opera days, I survived with a George Foreman grill (my capacity for voluntary suspension of disbelief makes infomercials a dangerous proposition!).

I would make a compact and beautiful kitchen. Would I love a chef's kitchen with a gigantic island and lots of gas burners? Yes. But for the price I'd choose a better location in a thriving city. Perhaps that chef's kitchen could go into a communal space off the rooftop lounge. We are doing just that at The Clifton.

If I had to make my ideal apartment in a small package, I'd make sure there was a great shower. A resonant, walk-in shower where you can sing your heart out. And the steam would sail into the room and keep it from being the arid desert-like experience many modern heating devices create.

My ideal apartment would have track lights in the living room and recessed lighting in the bedrooms. That way people could combine different kinds of light to create an ambiance of romance or study or humor, depending on their mood.

Should there be a true bedroom, or perhaps a rotated design like in Hyattsville to free up more space for the living room? I can live with that. Or perhaps the unit is a little larger and has an extra bedroom or den so people can share and save money. If you are trying to make housing affordable, you need to accept that there are trade-offs.

Here is the punch line of this chapter. This is the apartment that we've been trying to build all over the United States. With every project, we get closer and closer to the ideal of what will make people happy.

Of course, we learn from our mistakes. At The Bond, I thought it was a brilliant idea to carve out bedrooms wherever we could. In retrospect, I probably should have made more closets! After each project, we understand a little better how to deliver beauty without wasting money or space.

In Hyattsville, we have crafted an amenity package to provide meaning and pleasure to complement the efficient units, one that is in keeping with the renaissance of that neighborhood as an arts community. The first thing we did based on our HBS student feedback was to set aside a gigantic space for package delivery! In addition to a concierge, we have an Amazon locker system, refrigerated storage for grocery deliveries, a place to hang dry cleaning, you name it.

We also reutilized and reimagined existing spaces. A former entrance with three sides of glass and a skylight is becoming a Moroccan-inspired solarium, with turquoise tiles, lounge seating, and lots of greenery. Building on my father's tradition of taking inspiration from one's past, I'm pretty sure we'll be the only property in the neighborhood with one of those.

Inspired by the arts revival in downtown Hyattsville, we designed an artist and "maker" space, where adults or children can exercise their creativity. There's a whole movement of young people making their own bikes, mozzarella, lamps, furniture, and large-scale artwork. We wanted to give people a space in which to do that. We also have WeWork-style co-working offices on the ground floor for entrepreneurs pursuing their dreams in the building.

Our architect devised an "alone together" room based on his observation of the current cultural moment. He noticed that people love a place to sit with their laptops and do work, but they don't want to be totally alone. This room has intimate nooks and also long tables (with power outlets for laptops!) for people to work socially.

We also created a "rock star room," with an LP collection and a small stage for musical performances. This was inspired by the impact of music in my own life. I want to give people the same joy I found studying *bel canto* and doing operas in the dining hall, in a very affordable apartment building. I'm not sure if anyone will do opera in this room, but if the next Beatles are discovered in the building, you heard it here first!

I'm trying to put the fantasy apartment and humanistic design into action in Hyattsville, The Clifton, all of our projects. Each unit is lovingly designed for efficiency and delight, with a creative flair that we call soulful minimalism. My partner David and I probably went through fifty iterations of the floor plans. We sketched modifications on a napkin, on paper, tracing paper over the blueprints— whatever was available when we woke up in the middle of the night with another idea.

We are crafting small, beautifully designed apartments to fly solo or share. As frozen music goes, they're a bit less Wagner, more Rossini. We are discovering a generous amenity package to accompany them, one that captures people's imaginations, that fosters creativity, and that unfurls the joys of being around our fellow humans. That, and the largest package room in North America!

Love and Work

Freud famously said that what people need is love and work. Or maybe he didn't, but others have picked up those themes in his conception of psychology. And just as these are the keys to life, they are also the keys to great humanistic real estate. People are yearning for the elements humanity evolved to need—to love, work, find food, or enjoy human contact. A village met these needs, a community of people who are also seeking something. Cities can also meet these needs.

I have lived or worked in all sorts of real estate. I originally wanted to share a few thoughts on developing the different asset classes, the main food groups, of real estate: residential, office, industrial, hospitality. Investors like to view each one individually, each with its own intrinsic risk characteristics. Halfway in, I realized that the asset classes of real estate are deeply about the art of living and how we choose to organize our society.

Real estate is the spaces that we work in, where we find meaning in our jobs, maneuver merchandise, create products, play, enjoy parks, watch sports, sit in prison, and ultimately die. Real estate shapes our experience of life every step of the way, so it is fitting that a humanistic vision should guide the way we shape our real estate.

The modern American office is a death trap. You don't need to trust me on this one if you've spent any time in an office in your lifetime. It is set up so people basically sit in front of a computer. You can lose years of your life in a sedentary stupor talking to a computer instead of interacting with people and places. That's not "work." Work is toiling in the field, making something, talking to people, solving problems, making people happy, inventing new solutions. Most offices are computer-centric pressure cookers where stress and discomfort will slowly kill you.

We need a more humane view of office space so that people can find meaning in their work. When we set up Aria's offices, we used architecture to foster the things that we value most about work. We wanted a zen atmosphere for deep, patient thinking. We wanted a creative table where people could collaborate, brainstorm together, look at building plans, or just share a sandwich. On that table we held little competitions comparing the best pizzas in the neighborhood, or the best pastrami sandwich. It's still "the office," as opposed to a home or vacation spot. But it's a fun and sometimes inspiring place to be.

Sigmund Freud's office was filled with exotic, evocative anthropological relics. Freud thought people could access their subconscious minds better amidst symbols and mythology. So it occurred to me to try this in my own office to foster creativity. The same subconscious Freud sought in dreams or "Freudian slips"—why not make it a part of your daily work? Ask me about the scimitar on my shelf (a gift from Yigal), the nineteenth-century cast-iron ornaments, or the vintage door knockers!

Companies like WeWork are trying to make offices more fun and humane. Perhaps there's a Ping-Pong table and a place to have a beer together or to sit down with colleagues, like a living room. Whether WeWork is really worth $20 billion for basically managing offices based on "spiritual energy," that's another story. That's where the truth detector antennae from my banking days are alerted. Might as well enjoy the company for what it is—a terrific creative reinvention of the workplace.

I think offices should be human-centered. That means avoiding places where the computer is enthroned and people are bit players.

Robert Nozick, my professor of philosophy at Harvard, wrote about a hypothetical hedonism machine, a device you could attach yourself to that would give you pleasure, nonstop. You would never experience pain again. You would live only positive experiences through a machine. Would you choose that?

More and more of our work experiences are mediated by machines, social media, email, documents, Excel, and text messages. American teenagers spend six hours a day in front of a screen and send, on average, several hundred texts a week. Imagine how easy it is to find love, sex, business, money—all deliverers of primal brain chemistry like serotonin—online. But online doesn't have the authenticity of real friendship, sex, love, work. So, if you wouldn't even choose to live your life through the hedonism machine, where technology makes all your experiences pleasurable, why live your work life through a machine? There's hardly time left to learn and practice the Handshake Philosophy.

The other great workplace in America—industry—has been in a long decline. Industrial real estate once flourished in the cities of America. Garment manufacturing, meatpacking, haberdashery, shoe manufacturing, furniture making, diamond polishing—all occurred in the heart of cities. They added a diversity to the economic base and life options. In my first job, I saw lemon juice packaged in little yellow plastic lemons in a quirky factory built over decades, the fabrication of nondairy creamer in South Carolina, a high-speed assembly line churning out Frappuccinos for Starbucks in western Pennsylvania. You could tell from the pride in the eyes of the people working there that these plants really made the community.

America is still grappling with the impact of deindustrialization, economically and politically. I saw it in the fate of Lenox China and the reinvention of the Clairol factory. It's a reflection on the landscape of cities and ultimately the landscape of the American Dream. And the landscape of America and also the city I love are not always evolving in the right direction.

It would be incredible to bring industry back to the cities and landscapes where it once flourished. A young but optimistic cohort of makers is trying to do exactly this, revitalizing gigantic industrial spaces like the Brooklyn Navy Yard and Industry City. There is a whole maker movement being reborn out of the joy people are finding in creation and fabrication. American work is continually reinventing itself. I once sang *Don Giovanni* with the New Bedford Symphony, a town that lost its industry—whaling—a hundred years ago. If we simply lamented how whaling went into decline due to the introduction of electric lamps, we wouldn't have gotten very far. We have to put our shoulder into reimagining and reinventing meaningful work.

Ultimately the art of office and industrial real estate is creating a setting for people to find jobs and pursue meaningful work. America needs meaningful work and is lacking it. In earlier days, Americans farmed and were in touch with nature, herded cattle, worked machines, mined coal, traded merchandise, and bought and sold shares on the floor of the stock exchange. But now there isn't enough meaningful work.

We need visionary developers to polish our country like the jewel that it is. What if we turned that humanistic instinct of real estate development on the landscape today? What could we achieve? More affordable cities, more beautiful landscapes, more community and democracy and social harmony. People living and working more meaningful lives. More productive work. Less time commuting. More opportunities to connect to other people, find a mate, grow old together. We can't continue to throw up garbage that is an affront to nature. My adventures learning real estate development have made me wonder: Could we use a creative development mindset to make America, and perhaps even the world, a better place?

Some Thoughts on Growing Up in New York

My understanding of city life is heavily influenced by growing up in New York City in the 1970s and 80s. I grew up in a neighborhood where you never knew who could be sitting next to you. I once hopped on the bus coming home from school carrying my old violin case. My violin was a gift from my grandfather that had been bequeathed to him by a violin-maker tenant. A faded paper inside the body of the violin showed that it was made in Czechoslovakia in 1923. The case was weathered and seemed about that age too! I was approached by an elderly lady who was enthusiastic to hear that I was learning to play in an orchestra. She revealed that as a little girl she had been at a performance of Mahler's Second Symphony in Vienna—conducted by Gustav Mahler himself!

My neighborhood was filled with refugees from Europe, scholars, psychologists, musicians, and professors. People were excited about the humanities the way they are about technology today. It felt important and vital, part of a living tradition. Across town at my school, I found the same sense of wonder and intellectual engagement. My incredible teachers, raised in the open-minded 1960s, focused on independent exploration and discovery.

My closest friends, Daniel Petroff and David Zindel, also lived in the neighborhood. In those days, West Siders were considered edgy outsiders. Petroff had some wooden boards and milk crates at home that we used to build forts. He and I learned aikido at the West Side YMCA when our parents thought we needed to toughen up to get around town safely. With Zindel, we'd build gadgets, catapult fruit at neighboring apartments, rent action movies, drink Yoo-hoo, and throw a Frisbee around in Central Park. Occasionally we'd go crazy and go for a $4.75 lunch special at the Chinese restaurant around the corner.

Over time, our projects grew more complex and our excursions more elaborate. Petroff and I made some serious Jackson Pollock knock-offs. The three of us discovered new neighborhoods of New York City by trying to find the best slice of pizza in town (it might have been Di Fara's, but as kids we couldn't handle the hour wait while the owner lovingly put a sprig of basil on every pie).

At the same time, as rich as it was with the humanities and inner life, the city was dangerous. New York City had nearly gone bankrupt in 1975, the year I was born. Today, New York is held up as a paragon of a great city. But when I was growing up, New York felt like the train in *The Little Engine That Could* (a children's book I asked my mother to read to me so many times that I memorized it).

I remember school safety meetings where policemen briefed us on how to walk home: not too close to the cars or you could get kidnapped, but not too close to the buildings either, because someone might be lurking in the doorways! Don't wear or carry anything conspicuous. Keep $5 on you as "mug money" to readily give an attacker; that way people won't take your clothing or, worse yet, your life. My dad's Cutlass Ciera was stolen from in front of our house twice in a matter of two weeks. This was the era in which people put little humorous handwritten notes to would-be thieves on their windshields, saying, "No radio, already stolen."

I vividly remember the first time I felt safe in New York at night. I had just returned to the city after business school. I was walking down the street after getting a bite around the corner when it hit me that I wasn't experiencing fear. I was actually carefree and daydreaming and not looking behind me. It was a powerful realization.

Turns out freedom from fear is a good predictor of how people want to live. The decline in crime in American cities from 1995 to 2015 was a major contributor to the desirability of living in downtowns, and to investing in them. Physical safety is a key ingredient of a great location and a great city.

What a relief to be able to walk around my city without fear! Despite these changes, I still don't wear a watch. Truth be told, I tend to cast a glance behind me when walking out at night, wherever I am.

Most New Yorkers I know have a love-hate relationship with the city. We can't wait to get away, to the country, to the outdoors, to the mountains, or to another community. We long for nature, yet thrive among the cultural, artistic, architectural, and culinary joys of our home. As soon as we are gone, we start thinking about how we can get back. We have a hankering for that favorite pretzel or hot dog vendor.

Returning to the city after college, I was struck by the transformations taking place. Neighborhoods that were totally derelict were now havens for artists or young professionals. Areas that had been used for wholesale meatpacking, sweatshops, printing, prostitution, and rail yards had become apartments and offices, restaurants and bars and hotels. Neighborhoods were reborn.

The most powerful moment for me in New York was after September 11. I couldn't believe that anyone would do that to the city I loved. I joined crowds of people streaming into the streets to give blood, even though none was needed. Virtually no one in the twin towers when the planes hit had survived. I will never forget the smell of burnt flesh over Central Park, as I rushed across town to pick up my younger brother, and seeing the handmade missing-person posters attached to every fence. We didn't have the heart to admit to ourselves that the missing weren't coming back.

New Yorkers come together when the chips are down. Mayor Giuliani gave a speech at my synagogue reaffirming what it meant to be New Yorkers and Americans. We were in awe of the firefighters and policemen who had sacrificed everything to keep us safe.

Breaking the heart of New York City was something I will never forgive or forget. But they didn't break our spirit. People just wanted to be together and share their pain. The musical community came together in a powerful way. I remember going to Carnegie Hall with my uncle Jeffrey for a musical tribute. When the great American soprano Leontyne Price came out of retirement to sing "God Bless America," there wasn't a dry eye in the house.

Cities

A great city is a place where people can meet and fall in love, find meaningful work, and pursue their dreams. If Beethoven is the Romantic literature of nature, tango captures the spirit of cities. I fell in love with tango in my early twenties. I think it came from seeing *The Scent of a Woman* with Al Pacino with my first flame. Al Pacino plays a blind man who knows how to speak to a woman. I went gaga for the tango and learned to sing it. I discovered that tango was forged in the urban laboratory of Buenos Aires of the 1920s. It was centered on a neighborhood where all social classes mixed: Italian immigrants, gaucho cowboys, workmen, locals, and newcomers.

The language of tango is the language of love in an urban setting. Falling in love under the streetlamps with flirtatious neighborhood friends, betrayal at the horse-racing track, and other aspects of city life. In Beethoven, the natural landscape conjures romance. In *An die ferne Geliebte*, the singer implores nature to speak to his lover. In tango, you implore the city to speak to your beloved. The streetlights, the window where she first peeked out are your witnesses.

As a New Yorker, I can relate. Many of my first experiences in life were part of an urban landscape. When I sang Beethoven, I asked the clouds and the gurgling brook to call out to my beloved. But when I sang the *tango-canciónes* of Carlos Gardel, about his barrio and how it was silvered by the moon, I sang to the romance of the city.

A great city has to have a human scale. The superbroker of *Million Dollar Listing*, Ryan Serhant, tells a great story about how he got lost on the way to meeting his first client in Greenwich Village.

She didn't wait, hailed a cab, and left in a huff. But there was a deeper structure at work. Greenwich Village was laid out in the early nineteenth century as a separate town. Its street grid is all akilter. It meets the later, rectilinear New York street grid on various diagonals that no one can really figure out, even a real estate expert! But its human scale is why people love living there. It directly impacts property values. In real estate development, the urban design element is rarely emphasized, which is a mistake. It is vital to understand and utilize it.

Urban design is why the French quarter of Shanghai feels so different from the megablocks of Beijing. The organic, winding alleys of a medieval city feel very different from a planned nineteenth-century street grid or a twentieth-century sprawling city. The comparison is a human-scale street design versus one that is technological, authoritarian, or automobile focused.

Many cities of the twentieth century are designed around cars, and it's easy to feel that when you're there. They're not meant for walking. By contrast, organic, premodern city plans, like much of Boston or Greenwich Village, are amazing for pedestrians and street life. But they are terrible for cars. I once made one wrong turn trying to get to South Station in Boston. Everything there is one-way—the wrong way! I ended up circling around town for a half hour trying to get back to where I started.

Nothing against cars, which are a lot of fun to drive and absolutely essential in many places. Without driving, Mr. E might never have made it to America to chauffeur his brother and his bride to Niagara Falls. But cars can easily ruin the landscape and the sense of place people crave. Just as we seek a human-centric architecture as a real estate developer, we need a humanistic understanding of the city, how people want to live and work in an urban setting. In Gotham Center and Hyattsville, I've been able to participate in the rebirth of neighborhoods through people-focused development.

Sometimes the impact of a humanist approach is much smaller. When Aria was working on 321 Ocean, we had a small chance to make a difference. Unsightly overhead power cables ran in front of our building and the nearby park. We were not going to let Enrique's masterpiece be obscured!

We offered to have the lines buried on our part of the block. If you've ever tried to talk to the cable guy, try getting three different utilities, telephone, and cable providers to agree on relocating cables! But we persevered and spent a small fortune. Then we realized that we could do the same for the park! We proposed it to the city. We would take the same engineering and team and replicate the process. The city liked the idea so much, they decided to do it themselves! It was a minor gesture, and in the end we paid only for our corner and some engineering work. But no one else had ever done it.

At several other projects, we are filling in parking lots or former gas stations with pedestrian-friendly development. Little by little you can really repair the fabric of the city. My Florida and North Capitol development in DC combines one of each. My next idea is to re-create a nineteenth-century fountain that once stood nearby. It was demolished in an expansion of the interstate highway system without regard for the people who lived around it. The remnants of the fountain were recently discovered by some enterprising bloggers in a park at a military base. I don't know quite how, but I'm going to find a way to bring it back.

Building great cities takes patience and discipline. Look at the Herculean effort that was launched by the Bloomberg administration. It took decades to come to fruition, for the Prison Bus drop-off to become Gotham Center. As I was writing this book, Long

Island City's miraculous transformation came full circle! Amazon selected LIC as the site for one of its headquarters. That once-shunned industrial part of town became for a moment one of the business capitals of the world!

Then the deal collapsed, along with the chance to complete the transformation. Tons of great jobs in a neighborhood that really needed them.

Imagine if someone had done the kind of community work we had learned from Frank at 321 Ocean, and held some of the fifty-odd meetings we had organized at The Clifton. Imagine if all the parties had negotiated in good faith for a win-win solution. Job training for residents of the local Queensbridge Houses (the largest project in the city!), science and technology programs in local schools, a new park.

Imagine if someone had shown up personally with a crate of oranges as I did at The Alden, sat on the floor with residents of the Queensbridge Houses. Renovated a senior center nearby and bought laptops so local kids could learn computer science, as we did at The Clifton. A small gesture could have won priceless goodwill.

Maybe it was kismet; it was not meant to be. But in building great cities, sometimes you have to create your own destiny.

Building for the Middle

I still idealize the New York of my childhood, warts and all. But I'm afraid that it is becoming increasingly unaffordable, and it may be losing its hold on the popular imagination. Broadway was once the siren song that drew many to New York City. Then it was film and television. Woody Allen movies, *Seinfeld*, *Friends*—for decades people around the world imagined themselves young and in New York. Everyone laughed at New York humor. When *Sex and the City* came out, its salacious story lines gave audiences around the world a taste of the energy and quirks of living in New York. All of these shows were predicated on the assumption that young friendships and romances could blossom in New York. This was a place where people came to pursue their dreams as comedians, intellectuals, writers, PR executives, etc.

Maybe I'm a typical paranoid New Yorker, but it doesn't seem like there are many current TV shows that feature New York as a main character anymore! To flourish, New York must continue to attract the dreamers and teachers and songwriters and builders. In spite of its high prices, it must be attainable for people pursuing their passion.

And it's not just New York. In many ways, our greatest American cities are victims of their own success. Newly safe and flush with investment, they struggle to house the middle class. From the point of view of the builder, you basically have two choices—to build luxury apartments or federally subsidized low-income housing. The cost of land and construction make building for the middle extremely difficult. That's why you see so many luxury condominiums getting built, along with low-income housing.

Creative developers have a few tools at our disposal. Through special situations or adaptive reuse of older buildings, we can keep prices low enough to reach the underserved middle market. When we bought Vista 12 in Little Havana from its lender at 50 cents on the dollar, we could afford to rent it out monthly at $1.50 per square foot. This worked because we had purchased the building for far less than it would have cost to build today. But that doesn't work for new construction, on a scale that would make real estate more affordable.

I see higher density as a great way to match the preferences of millennials with the economic needs of middle-income development. Making spaces smaller enables us to offer a much lower absolute-dollar price point in great locations. Our approach of soulful minimalism—compact, efficient units that people love—could be part of the solution. Those small units are needed to make cities livable for young people.

Yet antiquated building and zoning codes have limited the size of apartment units. In many cities, including New York, you cannot legally build small units. Laws prohibiting them have been on the books since the time of tuberculosis-ridden tenements. Those codes need a makeover with our philosophy of soulful minimalism. But there are hidden prohibitions on soulful minimalism in all sorts of regulations, from rotated units to the size and shape of the kitchen to the number of people who can share an apartment. Outdated parking requirements make it cost-prohibitive to develop. People are flocking to our small units around the United States. That kind of unit should be permitted everywhere, to allow people of all income levels to enjoy the economic and social benefits of living in a great city.

In light of these obstacles, we have started to develop in new boroughs, former industrial zones, transit-accessible suburbs, and smaller cities. Many people were flabbergasted when AllianceBernstein recently moved 1,500 employees from New York to Nashville, Tennessee. The reality is that it has become prohibitive to enjoy a good quality of life in the biggest cities with an average American income. Our most recent project is the adaptive reuse of a historic athletic club and hotel into apartments in downtown Kansas City. The building features a ballroom, an Olympic-sized swimming pool, and a basketball court! It will offer affordable rental units and an exciting quality of life amidst a burgeoning tech scene and stable employment base.

The most powerful tool to create affordable housing is in the hands of public policy makers—public transportation. An extra subway stop can tunnel under the economic moats of the cities and whisk people to places where land and construction are less expensive. Residents can still be part of the same cultural sphere, have the same friends, and be part of the same place. Public transportation makes housing accessible to the middle class who cannot afford to live in the cities but cannot find well-paying, professional employment outside of them. After all, there is plenty of affordable housing in parts of the United States. You can buy a beautiful home for $100,000 in many places. It would just be hard to commute to work for a job 500 miles away! Public transportation is a great answer to this dilemma.

With all that we've got going for us in New York and the great cities of the United States, the secret to success in the next generation will be to create better opportunities for the middle class and creative professions. Policy makers have a huge opportunity to create affordability through better transportation, higher-density development, portability of government benefits, incentives for mixed-income housing, and continued reinvention of underutilized parts of town. With forethought and soulful minimalism, real estate developers could work hand in hand with policy makers to create less scarcity and more affordability in the best locations in the world.

There is much work to be done, and the challenges are daunting. Yet it's important to remember that this is not the first time people have feared New York City's demise. I was recently listening to the radio when highlights from *On the Town* came on. That's the 1949 musical starring Frank Sinatra and Gene Kelly that has the famous song "New York, New York." There is a whole bit where Sinatra, playing a sailor just back from the war, is hijacked by a female taxi driver who gives him a tour of the city.

Sinatra wants to see the great places his grandfather told him about. Each time he suggests a place, like the Woolworth Building, "the tallest building in the world," the taxi driver points out that it's either gone or eclipsed by something else! The Woolworth Building had been replaced by the Empire State Building as the world's tallest. The Hippodrome? Torn down years ago. "When was his guide book written?" she asks. 1905! When New York was truly great. So I guess we come by it honestly.

The city drew Frank Sinatra to see the Woolworth Building, and my grandfather to the Empire State Building, and me to Eleven Madison, one of the runners-up in the epic twentieth-century race to be the tallest skyscraper in the world. I hope New York will continue to grow and renew itself, and capture the imagination of Americans of all walks of life.

American Ideals

A family dinner at my grandmother's house would not be complete without giving thanks for living in America. Every get-together, over turkey or matzo ball soup, includes a prayer for our country and an expression of gratitude. Whatever we do in business, we are also part of the American community. America has welcomed my family and given us safety and opportunity beyond anyone's dreams. I've often found that America is poorly understood abroad. Today, I feel America is misunderstood even at home.

My grandmother Bernice is an inspiration to me in how to do the right thing and make a difference. She was born in Brooklyn during the Great Depression and grew up between New York and Arizona, where they thought her mother's asthma would be better. She married my grandfather when she was very young and raised a family for many years. Then she decided she wanted to build a life of her own. She found this spirit in nonprofit work and political activism.

Spending time with my grandmother is a lesson in American ideals. She loves our country. She is dedicated to the survival of the Jewish people. You never quite know who you are going to meet with her. I was once privileged to meet Congressman John Lewis, a true hero and a man of deep humility, who as a child in rural Alabama, learned public speaking by preaching to the chickens. With my grandmother, I always feel that there is hope, that our country can improve itself with devotion and hard work.

Lately it has felt as if prosperity and security haven't reached deep parts of the United States, and that's something to worry about. Most of the gains in the last several decades have gone to the top quintile and most successful parts of the country. That doesn't sit right. A lot of people are living their lives in fear and insecurity, which is evidenced by the rise in suicides and drug addiction. People are worried about their jobs, their healthcare, and their retirement. After all, you never know if you'll be born among the haves or the have-nots. You want to have a society that works for both, one that allows everyone to live in freedom from fear and reach their human potential.

Brazen falsehood is openly celebrated. This has led many people I care about into paroxysms of fury that the truth isn't being respected. And they're right to be upset. But my experiences suggest that while truth is important, people are also craving meaning, stories, a way to make sense of their lives. They also want goodness and beauty. People are not always rational economic actors. They go for the meaning and not the square footage. My sense is that the way out of the woods has to include elements of faith, goodness, poetry, patriotism, and idealism as well as truth and science. New leadership has to speak to the soul as well as addressing the mind.

The metaphor of the broken vase has been a unifying theme that brings together my life in real estate with opera, music, cities, and faith. Repairing what's broken around you and finding wholeness can be meaningful and compelling. If you can work even on a small scale toward repairing what's broken, righting a wrong, whether it's architecturally or through urban design, repairing a relationship or finding forgiveness, you are making the world whole again. It is one of the great things to strive for in your job on a small scale.

For me, working in the real estate business, this metaphor manifests itself in the repairing of the city. Weaving together pieces of the city that were torn asunder by highways or the urban renewal that destroyed Frank Del Vecchio's neighborhood. When we build contextual, urban infill buildings, we are slowly renewing the street life that makes a city great. We are helping to put the broken vase of the city back together. We can see this in the vibrant downtowns that are coming back to life in cities across America.

A lot of work remains to repair the broken vase of our communities. There are big divisions between rich and poor, city and country. In my journeys across America while I was singing opera, I was overwhelmed by the kindness and generosity of the communities I encountered. I saw the Handshake Philosophy reflected in small gestures and communities nationwide. Today, the American Dream sometimes feels like a broken vase that needs to be lovingly restored. It needs *e pluribus unum*. More than ever we need the practical, roll-up-your-sleeves ethos of soulful repair and wholeness.

The America that I believe in is the America of Ed Bavaria. Ed is a big, strong guy from Ohio who ran aircraft engines for GE before retiring in Sarasota, Florida. I got to know him while singing opera there under the baton of the Maestro. Ed is tough. But you should see him cry when he's listening to *Rigoletto*, where a father loses his daughter. I was once invited to Ed's house for a special dinner with some of the singers. Mrs. Bavaria had cooked all day to make delicious dishes for us. I saw them go out of their way to welcome everyone and make people feel at home, regardless of race, religion, or creed. In other countries I've occasionally had the opposite experience. But not in America.

I recently sat down with Frank, the idealist and civic activist. I found him disillusioned. He was concerned that America is losing its way. I hear where he is coming from. But I believe we have the potential to get back on track. I've seen the potential for transformation in real estate development, how vision and perseverance can change something and make it better. Perhaps it's odd coming from a real estate developer, but that's where I've learned local politics,

Athenian democracy, and the struggle to make a small bit of earth better. Look at America as a real estate development that we have to build. We have to show it love, work with communities, seek truth, beauty, and goodness.

The power of real estate development is the power to see potential. It gives you the ability to transform a place with dreams and inspiration. One good turn can beget another. In renovating The Alden and treating people with respect, we found The Clifton. We got to put forth a lot of love, and work with tenants as people. With inspiration and a bit of soil, along with input from the community, we have been able to realize a small piece of the American Dream, for ourselves and others.

The America that I love can be found in many places and in small gestures. I encountered it in a waitress in a luncheonette when I was about five. Mr. E and my uncle Donald had taken me along on a trip to Washington. We ate lunch at a counter in a diner and spent the day touring the town. We marveled at its spotless subways. Then we realized that Mr. E had lost two raw diamonds that were in his breast pocket! Mr. E was always helping someone out in his own way, and he had probably bought them for someone's engagement ring and was planning to have them polished and set. But the diamonds were lost! He must have dropped them when he took his reading glasses out of his pocket. We retraced our steps and circled back to the diner. The waitress went to the back and brought out the two valuable diamonds intact. She had found them and kept them for us!

I remembered this years later in the real estate business when I found a man who kept his word despite being offered millions more for his buildings on Crosby Street. I thought about it when I met a public servant who sacrifices everything for his neighborhood and community, Frank Del Vecchio. I'm lucky to be part of the America of Bernice, the Maestro, Miss Peggy, Mr. E, Peter, Sam Sakarian, Frank Del Vecchio, and other great Americans I've met. I hope to do right by them.

Building Your Sistine Chapel

Building your Sistine Chapel is my metaphor for making something and exercising your creativity in work. It can be physically creative, like repairing bicycles or making chicken marsala, or it can mean using your imagination to create something at work. A new idea, a new way of doing things, a new app or website. For me it was restoring every mortar joint in The Alden with lime-based plaster. It is exercising creativity in what we build.

My second-grade teacher was obsessed with the Italian Renaissance. She had us construct a replica of Renaissance Florence out of painted milk cartons and other household objects. A two-liter Coke bottle served as the Duomo. We set up a fair in which we each adopted a period profession, and we minted gold leaf coins out of clay to use as currency.

One day, we went to the art room where we learned how to make plaster frescoes in shoe box tops. Our teacher then had us tape them to the bottoms of our chairs. What on earth was the purpose of taping plaster to the bottoms of our seats? She had us paint the plaster while lying on our backs—to experience how Michelangelo must have felt when painting the ceiling of the Sistine Chapel!

Michelangelo's work was completed over a period of thirty-four years. He spent some of the best years of his life on a rickety scaffold, alone, with paint falling on his face. When we develop a building, we put all the love we can into it, as if we are creating our own Sistine Chapel. We lavish attention on every aspect of a project.

Taking joy in the physical transformation of a property, or in the creation of anything in your work, is allowed. It's a key part of fulfillment. Make something beautiful. Don't be afraid. Don't say you are not a creative person. Everyone is a creative person; it's part of our human endowment. It just has to be expressed. It can start small.

This is not just meaning for the sake of meaning, which is art. It's meaning for the sake of business and making people happy. If you delight your customers by humanizing their experience of life's necessities, you are bound to succeed as a businessman.

I am still a businessperson and an investor who believes in value. Yet all of the human comedy—love, death, marriage—takes place in the real estate you make. For me, the ability to do something creative for other humans while still staying true to my principles, that's the secret of real estate development.

When it came time to construct 321 Ocean, we were filled with anticipation. Our hopes were high that we would build something beautiful, a place people really wanted to be. A lot of development occurs before a single shovel is placed in the soil. The concept, capturing the special charm of the location in your business plan—all occur in the mind and on paper before development begins. Then you have to go out and build it.

Banks were not exactly lining up to lend on a condominium project in Florida. Some of our existing lenders said no. But we did get one good proposal from a plucky bank in Arkansas called Bank of the Ozarks. They were just starting to venture out from their base in Texas and Arkansas and were open to doing the loan. We had to guarantee 35 percent of the loan balance personally. That certainly puts the fear of God into you!

It was the bank's first condominium loan in the state of Florida, which meant a lot of complex legal negotiations. We met with the head of real estate lending, Dan Thomas. Dan presents himself with an "aw shucks" manner as a farm boy, but he is also fiercely smart and knew every loan in his entire $5 billion loan book by heart.

After some brief pyrotechnics while we negotiated the loan documents, we were able to shake hands on the deal and close the loan.

Then we set out to build it. We drove piles deep into the sand to build a firm foundation. We poured the concrete shell over steel cables and rebar. We used a special architectural concrete so that Enrique's cylindrical columns could be exposed, a beautiful modern touch. We dug a pool next to the beach so that people could enjoy alternating between the two. We put in lush greenery to soften the modernism and reflect the climate.

Real estate development draws forth the best of partnership. Working together with David and Tim, friends since childhood, was a thrill. We worked hard and persevered through the inevitable setbacks. When our work was complete, we watched with joy as mothers played with their children in the pool and in the beautiful courtyard that we had fought for.

The Clifton presented another site with tremendous potential that we wanted to live up to. After working with forty-nine rent-controlled tenants and navigating the community process, it was time to build it. There were inevitable mishaps. During demolition, the facade of the charming building that we wanted to preserve became destabilized. The facade had a beautiful running bond, a brick pattern. As I've learned now, more than once, a beautiful running bond facade means that none of the bricks is rotated to tie the facade to what's behind it! We had to nail, board, glue, and tape our facade in place.

There were other setbacks. The zoning order was appealed by a neighboring condo association that had not participated in the two-year civic process. After some legal back-and-forth, we met over breakfast and worked out a solution.

We weren't able to fulfill the dream for all of the residents of the building. While we were fighting the appeal, one older resident had to go into a nursing home. She didn't make it. We are praying for the remaining tenants and getting closer to bringing them back to their apartments by the day!

Everyone has to paint their own Sistine Chapel, do something personally meaningful that involves sacrifice. The creativity of making something taps into a very powerful part of the brain and awakens the soul. Let it be a garden that you tend with care, or a tree house that you build for your kids, or a special touch on a website or product. Let it be something at work where you add a little bit of yourself to what you're doing, to what you're making. There is a spark of divinity in creation, even in a tiny gesture. It is an essential and fulfilling part of whatever you do, from finance to carpentry.

We each have to do our small part to paint this magnificent country on our backs. Make a small corner of the city better. Make our designs and landscape and cities and suburbs and farms more human. Take down the power cables, break bread together on the floor, bring forth some love for our fellow man where it's needed. Take care of those who are in despair, save a little bit of nature. I know I'm not completely crazy because I've seen it happen little by little.

I recently brought my family to The Clifton in DC to take part in building my labor of love. We each got to take a few bricks and mortar them into place. Then we learned that the mason had to do several thousand a day! My respect goes to the masons who work tirelessly to build something beautiful.

Every brick that we lay brings us closer to the day when I get to welcome Miss Peggy to her new home. Real estate development can give us some of the joy of making something and the privilege of serving others. Done right, it lets us lay one small brick in making the world a better place.

PART IV

The Future
of Real Estate

Coda

We were getting ready to publish this book when the unthinkable happened. Covid-19 took our cities and the world by storm. Within months, we had witnessed events not seen in the United States for a hundred years. Record unemployment and bread lines. Midtown Manhattan a ghost town. National borders closed. Our American politics a wreck.

It's hard to overstate what a fall this was from the optimistic end of the book. It was tragedy and pain on a scale I had not seen in our country. On a national level, it was an outbreak of disease and suffering that laid bare cracks in our democracy and wrenching inequality. On a personal level, many of the things I believed in and cared about were called into question. How can you embrace humanistic values and the Handshake Philosophy when you can't touch another person? How can cities work their magic when you can hardly leave the house?

My first instinct was to help however I could. I joined with my business partners and friends to support food deliveries, community centers, restaurants, and arts organizations. We checked in on elderly folks in our buildings. Miss Peggy, who by now was happily living in her new apartment in The Clifton, had a close brush with Covid. She made it. Eighty years old and blind, she still manages to bring joy and spirit to each day.

Sarasota Opera, home to Maestro DeRenzi of previous chapters, had to cancel the end of the season. But they made the choice to continue paying the singers, musicians, carpenters, electricians, and costume makers, who would have been hurting. To me, that was an inspiring act of fundamental decency that today seems all too rare. It was the values of the Handshake Philosophy in action.

I tried to be Superman—Superdad—holding up my family and colleagues while trying to help all the communities we work in. I was able to hang in there until the fall. Then I learned what tying your passion to your business, as I have advocated in these pages, can mean when things get tough! It has been gut-wrenching to watch the cities I love deteriorate, in most cases while I am powerless to help. Now that there is a light at the end of the tunnel, we have to begin rebuilding, and we must build back better.

I believe the values and concepts in the book transcend any particular time period. When the dust settles, those will remain. But Covid has certainly turned the world upside down. We need to understand which changes might have a lasting impact on the fabric of our society—how we live and work—and which are fleeting reactions to the pandemic. Some of the important changes that appear to be wrought by Covid may turn out to be a hastening of trends that were already well underway. The purpose of Part IV is to examine the impact of Covid-19 and the technological changes it has accelerated on the real estate world. As I write this, we are still in the fog of war. It's hard to see where things will lead. Please view these preliminary observations as food for thought. Lord knows things can change rather dramatically!

This is ultimately an idealistic book, firm in the belief that businesspeople guided by humanistic values can make a difference. This new section gives us the opportunity to have a brief glimpse of emerging dynamics in the realms of geography, technology, and cities. By trying to make sense of these real-time changes, however imperfectly, we can begin to sketch out what rebuilding after the pandemic could look like, and we can take action to make things better.

Geography

Location, location, location. The three most important factors to consider in real estate. But the oldest joke in the book of course contains more than a grain of truth. In previous chapters, we have examined what constitutes a great location, the rise and fall of neighborhoods, and how location sealed the divergent fates of Lenox China and the Clairol headquarters. We have explored the enchanting urban environments whose combination of work, friendship, food, music, and human connection have for decades drawn people to the heart of the city.

What happens if you suspend location as the main principle of real estate?

Taking some poetic license, Covid-19 simulated this effect for many white-collar employees. Suddenly, you're barely allowed to leave the house. You can't physically go to the office or school. You can't see friends or go to restaurants or stores or concerts. In some cases, you could be anywhere. As long as you have high-speed internet, for those fortunate enough to be able to work from home, the role of location as a meaningful positive in your life is significantly diminished.

In recent years, city center locations have attracted insatiable demand and premium rents. But without the magic of location, people leave. When offices, restaurants, and cultural attractions didn't reopen last fall, brutal job losses and the suspended appeal of city living contributed to a changed landscape. Many millennials left big cities for smaller ones or more reasonably priced suburbs. As of last fall, more than half of eighteen to twenty-nine-year-olds were living with their folks, the highest level since the Great Depression.

We experienced this dynamic firsthand. For a while, the Washington, DC, market held up exceptionally well. With its abundance of government offices, universities, and growing tech and services employment base, DC had shown incredible resilience in the Great Recession. For a time, we thought we'd dodged a bullet. Then all hell broke loose. When jobs and schools in the city didn't open as expected in September, many residents moved out. It was a real business challenge on a scale we hadn't faced in a long time. What felt like value investment pre-Covid wasn't quite as clear once what makes a great location was in doubt!

The key components of a great location—a place where you can find a job, friendship, or love—have been suspended by the coronavirus. For now, the key to a good life is fresh air, a little sunshine, and more space. Where can you get a lot of space for not as much money? It sure isn't New York! Thus began the cottage industry of predicting the end of the city.

On August 13, 2020, James Altucher, one of the owners of the Stand Up NY comedy club in my old neighborhood, published a piece on his LinkedIn account entitled "NYC Is Dead Forever. Here's Why." It went on to lament the conditions of lockdown in New York, depicting a death spiral of fleeing businesses, shuttering cultural institutions, and declining quality of life. "People say, 'NYC has been through worse' or 'NYC has always come back,'" wrote Altucher. "No and no." This was truly the end. No matter how much one may love New York and never say die, everything was going the wrong way according to Altucher. This time was different.

And then came Altucher's coup de grâce: the impact of technological change in the form of high-quality bandwidth. New York City would never be the same, he argued, because of the explosive growth in bandwidth speed as average speeds increased from three megabits per second in 2008 to twenty per second today. As a result of that change, reliable, high-quality video and Zoom calls became possible. All of history can now be divided into before and after remote work. "People have left New York City and have moved completely into virtual worlds . . . Wall Street can now stretch across every street instead of just being one building in Manhattan," Altucher concludes. "That's what is different."

To the great amusement of many readers, Jerry Seinfeld decided to chime in. He was not buying it. He appealed to readers by citing timeless human values that have made cities gathering places over millennia. And he was not impressed by the bandwidth argument.

In an article called "So You Think New York Is 'Dead' (It's not.)," Seinfeld took to the pages of the *New York Times* to counter Altucher's argument with his own take on technology and human nature. He rejected the notion that, if given the choice, people would work remotely. "Guess what: Everyone hates to do this. Everyone. Hates. You know why? There's no energy," wrote Seinfeld. No fiber optic cable could transmit the energy and attitude that define New York.

He went on to ask why people cluster in cities or regions like Silicon Valley, when they could be anywhere and connect through their devices. It doesn't work, he argued, because it's missing the energy, the creativity, the innovation. "Real, live, inspiring human energy exists when we coagulate together in crazy places like New York City . . . You think Rome is going away too? London? Tokyo? The East Village? They're not. They change." Great cities adapt and thrive. Bringing creative people together in the same physical place fosters business and innovation.

Who's got it right? I tend to think, paraphrasing Mark Twain, that rumors of the city's demise are greatly exaggerated. To me, Seinfeld's argument rings true. Cities will survive and flourish in the future. Despite current pain, cities fulfill certain essential human

needs. Industries cluster in certain cities and regions to foster innovation. And no amount of technology can substitute for human
interaction. For every family fleeing the city for greener pastures,
there are probably as many millennials or Generation Z "zoomers"
desperate to get out of their parents' houses as soon as possible! The
drop in rents makes New York and other big cities more affordable
to those fortunate enough to have work. Once the fear of illness
or death subsides, cities will flourish once again. We saw that after
September 11. The Roaring Twenties followed on the heels of the
Spanish Flu. But what if some life choices are driven by technologies that will forever alter the way people live?

Elements of this polemic remind me of the tongue-in-cheek
debate between Elon Musk and Warren Buffett we examined in
earlier chapters. Timeless values and human nature versus brash
futurism and technology. Just with more comedy. While there's
something viscerally satisfying about Seinfeld telling the other
guy to be fruitful and multiply—only not in those words!—and
championing the passion and energy of New York, the bandwidth
argument raises important questions that we will need to examine
more closely.

Technology

To understand the impact of technology on the future of real estate, we need to look to the past. In each generation, technology has interacted with geography to shape human society and its real estate. Covid has accelerated the rate of technological change and the transformation of real estate.

With a little imagination, the impact of technology on the cities and real estate of America can be read plainly on the map. In a highly stylized version of American geography, ships gave rise to the coastal cities and river towns, the railroad opened up the middle of the country, the invention of the elevator made the skyscrapers of New York possible, the automobile produced Los Angeles, and air conditioning made Las Vegas, Miami, and Houston possible. With some indulgence for this sweeping historical oversimplification, we can see how new technologies have shaped society and real estate.

The Information Age—characterized by computers, the internet, email, and mobile phones—has radically transformed society and the way we organize our time. According to a recent study by Nielsen, Americans spent more than twelve hours a day consuming media in the first quarter of 2020, much of it online. But in many ways, the physical real estate we inhabit remains shaped by history and adapted to previous eras.

Our cities retain the vestiges of the organic medieval town center, nineteenth-century urban planning, and automotive commuting. They are filled with offices that hold reams of documents as well as people, and shops full of inventory. As we have discussed in this book, Amazon, Google, and Facebook were already shaping how we read and how we shop, how we remember and how we socialize. Large swaths of commercial real estate that are adapted to that old economy are at risk of becoming obsolete. While home prices shot up double digits across the United States, the value of commercial real estate took a major hit.

What will happen when we suddenly jump seven years into the technological future, as a survey of American corporations recently characterized the acceleration of their adoption of information technology due to Covid? How will our cities adapt, and how will it impact real estate values and development?

Industrial real estate is on a tear—not necessarily to build things, but to distribute them. Remember the Lenox China facility, where long ago I learned the hard way that a changing economy had rendered certain kinds of industrial real estate obsolete? Online shopping and shipping have reversed this dynamic. Amazon has challenged retail and made industrial real estate a safe haven!

The tectonic changes we are exploring raise a much larger question about the nature of human experience—will real estate be superseded by technology? Is there a seismic shift in the experience of life between in-person life, mediated by real estate, and virtual life, mediated by technology? This is a different question than whether or not the city is dead. This is about whether real estate as a means of mediating human interaction will be replaced by technology.

There is certainly data that supports the hypothesis. People spend hours on their devices and now Zoom every day, in place of human interaction in physical space. People find work, food, shopping, romance, sex, entertainment, art, and knowledge online.

The weighted composition of the S&P 500 also reflects that transformation. Where real world industries, including manufacturing, materials, and natural resources once dominated, the market capitalizations of the world's largest companies are now heavily weighted toward a growing legion of tech companies. And perhaps this is justified? If people shop at Amazon instead of at a mall, it stands to reason that the role of technology in mediating human exchange will rise, and that of physical space will fall. In a changing of the guard between the Information Age economy and the old economy, the physical world is losing out to the digital world.

The most powerful catalyst for change may be the ubiquitous Zoom. The office has been a prodigious force in the organization of cities for over a century, although as we have seen in earlier chapters, the modern office experience leaves much to be desired. The pandemic has temporarily compelled many of us (especially those fortunate enough to be able to stay at home during the most perilous periods) to work from home. What will it do to real estate and cities if working from home—or living at work as some humorists have described it—becomes widespread?

Some of the first clues to this trend—whether short term or sustained—started to emerge from our online apartment listings. I like to post Craigslist ads myself for our properties, to have my finger on the pulse of what the customer wants. It helps me make decisions about the next crop of apartments we are designing.

As the coronavirus hit, the most popular ad in my roster was "Exquisite Junior One Bedroom with Balcony!" The second most clicked was "Brand New Junior One Bedroom with Balcony!" You get the idea. People were still cost-conscious and wanted a great price point. But if they were going to spend hours per day on phone calls or staring at a laptop, they prized the ability to swing open their doors and spend time outside.

What were the biggest changes in what people looked for in an apartment in 2020? Thanks to search technology, we can find out. Evidently, stationary biking while working from home to the scent of freshly baked bread was what excited people during the waves of lockdowns. *The Real Deal* published an article based on StreetEasy renter searches in New York City. Peloton bikes shot up in popularity, as did searches that contained the word "baking." Listings that mentioned home offices quadrupled, so unless the inventory changed dramatically, rooms that had once been intended for roommates or children in a tighter market were reimagined for work. As I had seen in my Craigslist listings, searches for outdoor space also spiked.

I believe that residential real estate will have to morph and expand to serve a broader set of human needs. When residential real estate was deemed "essential" while offices, stores, and hotels were closed, apartments remained open to give people a home. Residential took on the functions of almost every kind of real estate. Lobbies receiving an enormous volume of packages replaced retail, broadband for work from home replaced offices, and roof decks and outdoor spaces for fresh air and a "staycation" replaced hotels. Suddenly our residential properties were doing the work of all of the asset classes combined! Residential real estate is in the midst of its own transformation to provide what we have termed in this book "low cost with meaning." Apartments must give people a newly expanded vision of essentials in walkable neighborhoods at a reasonable price, in the context of dramatically changing technologies.

One solution may be to find ways to let technology tap into our humanity. In earlier chapters, we discussed how Steve Jobs infused his early Apple computers with a human-centric desktop interface and offered a panoply of calligraphy-inspired fonts. Zoom technology has fostered parent-child playtime by reducing commuting, dating sites have helped us find true love, and Netflix and others have brought great storytelling on demand into our homes. This book has chronicled our efforts to humanize the apartment and the experience of city living, to adapt our buildings to how people want to live and deliver meaning and joy at a reasonable price. Perhaps the next great innovations will harness technology and real estate to make our lives better.

On a more granular level, we have been experimenting with innovations in proptech and AI to deliver a better residential experience to our tenants. Our arialiving.com website is mobile friendly and employs chatbots with artificial intelligence and videography to make it easier for someone to find an apartment. Our Nest "learning" thermostats adapt their temperatures to mimic people's behavior over time, making residents comfortable while saving energy. A "transit screen" in the lobby of new buildings advises residents of when the next subway or bus is coming. In many small ways, we are using technology to make the residential experience more natural and intuitive, as well as more climate friendly.

I don't think that tech-mediated life will supersede place-mediated life. But to compete for people's attention, we have to make incredibly compelling places, filled with beauty and the potential for meaningful contact. We must preserve nature, bring it into our cities, and preserve wilderness wherever we can. We have to make our cities jewels that can stand up on their own. Part of why people have turned away from physical experiences may be because we have defaced so much of the earth with meaningless sprawl, the destruction of wildlife, and a proliferation of cars, so that it is no longer recognizable as home to our ancient human brains.

The potential for change in our industry is truly exciting when real estate is reimagined in light of new technologies to serve a more humanistic vision. A transformed real estate landscape could make work more fulfilling. Offices would remain an important part of the business experience, but deals could also be made in parks, over coffee, on Zoom, on a street corner, or on a hiking trail. A wave of office and hotel conversions to thoughtfully designed apartments would mean many more people could walk to work (or Zoom to international meetings). With less commuting and less frenetic travel, there would be less strain on the environment and more time for relationships. I found glimpses of this experience in the precious time spent with my own family while working from home during the pandemic. But this positive vision of technological change is not a sure bet. It depends on the success of public policy, which we will delve into more deeply in the next chapter.

The Soulful City

If there is room for optimism amidst the coronavirus tragedy, it is in the hope that the current technological and social challenges will spur great cities to reinvent themselves, to deliver on the unbelievable potential of city life. This crisis gives us both the opportunity and the obligation to rebuild the great cities of America, and we must rebuild them better.

I experienced firsthand what great cities can do. I stepped into a cab and discovered kismet. I got to start my career and find mentorship in finance, opera, and real estate. Only in New York!

But it's hard to imagine all this happening today. We can hardly keep up with the major challenges that keep piling up. And the coronavirus crisis has laid bare the cracks in our foundation.

Bringing back our great cities as engines of opportunity is one of the foremost challenges of our time. Reflecting on my life and experiences, I see four areas of investment and action that would help bring New York City and the great cities of America back. These are a few ideas—not a comprehensive prescription for public policy. They are not a panacea for the major challenges of jobs, health care, inequality, climate change, and quality of life. Rather, they are idiosyncratic ideas based on my direct experiences meant to complement a more expansive public policy. Perhaps they will constitute a tiny piece of the puzzle of how to make a more just and beautiful city.

Embrace Housing Biodiversity

We need to address affordability and create mixed-income, mixed-use, intergenerational neighborhoods. As we discussed in Building for the Middle, developers have essentially two choices—build class A expensive apartments or build federally subsidized low-income housing. There's no in-between. This makes for a tale of two cities. Housing monoculture—whether for rich or poor—isn't good for anyone.

This can be addressed by embracing what I call housing biodiversity. We need a mixture of family apartments, microunits for young single people, co-living, rooming houses, and senior living. A mixture of incomes and generations living together in the same buildings, in the same neighborhoods. That's what made the West Side great.

Today, a legal and regulatory thicket makes it impossible to build efficient apartments to meet the diverse needs for reasonably priced housing. Regulations that have accumulated over generations shape what can and cannot be built. Some laws passed in reaction to the pandemic of 1918 are still on the books!

Why not make it legal to creatively use small spaces? Why regulate to the inch how people have to live? Why mandate huge ADA kitchens in every unit in a city where people love eating out—which keeps small businesses alive? Why regulate what light and air constitutes a bedroom, where across the country people are getting creative about sleeping quarters to drive down housing costs? Code-compliant new apartments are so great that no one can afford to live in them.

One example—why do you have to include kitchens to get a residential Certificate of Occupancy in hotels? Reviving hotels as apartments without kitchens would offer efficient, affordable units and provide much-needed jobs to restaurant workers who could reactivate shuttered hotel restaurants and bars. There are a lot of concerns about young newcomers moving into established neighborhoods and raising the rents. Accommodating more young professionals in converted hotels—or newly constructed smaller units that are presently illegal—would relieve some of the pressure on the remainder of the housing stock, and stands to make housing more attainable for all.

A plethora of obsolete office buildings and hotels could be converted right now to apartments and would transform the face of cities across America. With beautiful mixed-use, mixed-income neighborhoods, more people could walk to work. Cities across the world are embracing the idea of "the fifteen-minute city," where all the essentials are within a quarter-hour walk. This would be an important step toward fulfilling that aspiration. While the virus is wreaking havoc on our aging public transportation infrastructure—which desperately needs long-term investment and support—this would be an immediate shot in the arm. Cities would come back to life. In an era of climate change, less commuting would be a huge win for quality of life and for the environment.

Let Music Play On

We need to invest in music and the performing arts. This will require a lot of creativity and a lot of investment. Why are large industries bailed out, but artists and musicians are left for dead? These are the people who make us laugh or cry and feel human. How can we keep them going for a year or two? In many European countries, opera houses have opened with social distancing and other precautions. How can we create safe concerts to give people a chance to practice their craft? How can we create an ecosystem of artist housing so people have a place to live that's reasonably priced? Think about how it feels to walk through the streets and hear a solo saxophone playing "My Funny Valentine." Let's invest in safe concerts, street music, and Central Park performances, and most importantly in safely reopening performing arts venues. Without music, the city is dead.

More Streets for People

We need a new era of creative urban design and parks to encourage walking, nurture neighborhoods, and democratize city living. Central Park was created as a great democratic experiment—a natural place as grand as any English manor but free for all to enter and find refuge in the heart of the city. As we have discussed, that's why there are no elaborate gates. The creators of the park wanted anyone to walk in and feel at home.

In the great reshuffling of the city that's about to take place as geography adapts to technology, offices will become residences, hotels will become offices, people will work from home, and the whole economic order of the city will be recast. Let's try to do it to enhance the neighborhood as the unit of organization. That's what makes New York so terrific. If people can live and work in the same neighborhood, so much the better.

We have to reclaim the streets for people. We need a human-centric city. A recent study in the *New York Times* showed that roughly one third of the city's land area is taken up by roads, parking, and places for cars. Pedestrians are relegated to small sidewalks.

What if Broadway became a walking park, flanked by outdoor cafes and theaters? An unconventional path that has always marched to the beat of its own drummer, Broadway winds its way from the bottom to the top of Manhattan and beyond. With all the bike trails and pedestrian plazas, it barely serves for vehicular traffic anymore. Sidewalk restaurants have sprung up all across the city.

Great cities have beautiful walks. Romantic walks. Business walks. I know businesspeople who do their meetings on walks so

THE FUTURE OF REAL ESTATE

they don't sit at a desk all day! People who walk live longer. Let's restore broad swaths of the city to shoe leather. It will make the city much more livable.

Build the Next Generation of Builders

We need a new form of inclusive business education, to embrace all of our society. Business, industry, creativity, and technology will need to be part of the solution. We need a way to bring in the talent that exists and to teach young people how to use their talents in a meaningful way. Business can be a force for good and can make a difference in people's lives. I have built many luxury homes, and those are a lot of fun, but the most meaningful work has been making creative use of unappreciated and misunderstood raw materials, turning them into places for people to live a big life in the city at a lower cost.

There is already a movement afoot to do this. Project Destined is bringing diverse high schoolers, college students, and veterans who might never have had the chance to learn the real estate business into the fold. I had a chance to work with a group of interns from Howard University last fall, which culminated in a live business plan competition. The level of passion for real estate and thoughtful preparation was inspiring—and bodes well for the future of our industry. We who are part of design and development, construction and finance, help shape and build the city. We need to ask ourselves: What kind of a city do we want to build?

I think we know in our hearts what it will take to get New York and other great cities back. It will take patience. It will take love. It will take a lot of work—private sector, philanthropic, thought leadership, government. This is a hard time, but also a time of renewal and hope. By taking a small step to make our cities better and more livable, you never know if you might be opening the door to the next person pursuing their dreams.

New York, March 2021

Epilogue

We've come to the end of the journey. I've been on the lookout for the philosopher's touchstones of truth, beauty, and goodness in business across America and the world. From time to time I've had glimpses of them. I've found them in people, places, buildings, and communities, and I've even gotten the chance to contribute a few bars of my own.

My journey in the world of real estate has taken me through moments of flourishing and moments of difficulty and despair. It has forced me to find the courage to invest in the face of fear. It has taught me to stand up for others, to stand up for myself, and to uphold principles I believe in. I've gotten knocked down and learned from my mistakes. I've enjoyed the taste of exhilaration with partners and comrades-in-arms.

There's a riveting passage in Tolstoy's *Anna Karenina* where the philosophical gentleman farmer, Levin, picks up a scythe and harvests wheat for hours alongside forty-two other men. He is truly in his element and finds fulfillment. In our story, I think of Mr. E hunting for bargains and fixing things that were broken. How he taught me to wash a car with elbow grease and to put my heart into it with pride. I think of Oseola McCarty, who did her washing by hand and gave her life savings to provide opportunities for college students in her community. I think of Frank Del Vecchio, who dedicates his days to righting wrongs, standing up for fairness and the democratic process.

Each of these individuals derived meaning and joy from their work. But meaning and joy are not always easy to find in business. They require tapping into your deepest values, and putting your hands and heart and soul into your work. In work today, we are often tempted to bring only one aspect of ourselves to the office or cubicle, factory or store or field. In some jobs, it's our brain and logic; in others it's our physical prowess. Sometimes it's a gift for connecting to people. In some cases, it's creativity. But rarely are we called upon to use all of these aspects of ourselves in our work. And I feel we leave a lot of human potential on the table as a result. I hope this book has provided a few clues on how to bring your whole self to work.

Perhaps in selecting these stories I have painted too rosy a picture of the business! I could write another entire book chronicling all the bad things I've experienced in real estate. I'd have chapters on backstabbers and bullies, people who lie to you and betray your trust. There would be copious sections on con artists, charlatans, people who talk a big game, who swindle other people out of their money, who don't care about the neighborhood, who don't treat other humans with respect. I've experienced each of these personally.

I've seen how real estate can pull families apart. How it can destroy brotherhoods and partnerships and friendships. How sometimes the more money you have, the more fighting there is between good people. I've watched and wished I could help as big institutions lost tons of money they needed for their pensioners. As grand dreams collapsed or people were sold a bill of goods. But I've fought to do better and overcome these obstacles every day.

There needs to be a national conversation about what it means to be a businessman in America, and to be a real estate developer. What it means to be mentored or to apprentice with someone. It has to teach you how to be a human in your work. To work with grace, humility, and emotional generosity. Never to treat people poorly and hurt those weaker than you. Never to hit a man while he's down.

When I make an investment in a building or a piece of land, I do it as a businessman, not as an artist or a saint. What I do has to make money, hopefully a lot of it, and equally important, it has to avoid risk. Investing wisely is a responsibility that I take really seriously. But you have to do it with authenticity, honesty, and respect.

You never know how much time you have left on this earth. But I do have a few things left to do if I'm lucky enough to have the opportunity to do them. I have a lot more exciting deals up my sleeve. I have my pickax and shovel ready to dig up more arcane and abstruse structures that need fixing. There's always a cycle in real estate, and there will always be change. Who knows where the next chapters will come from, or where they will lead.

Maybe I'll hit the road and discover new parts of America. Or go international to new corners of the world. Perhaps I'll create a long-term investment vehicle to invest in patient deals that others aren't interested in. I'm tempted to create a residential brand with my own ethos, a little bohemian with great locations and buildings with character. Project Destined has created a meaningful and effective way to mentor young people in my field. I plan to do more to make sure the Handshake Philosophy continues into the next generation.

If I'm lucky I'll get to write two or three more books, about family legends and the etymology of the human heart, great human mysteries. Sing a few more bars and make people happy, or learn to conduct an orchestra and make music the way I believe it should be made. Maybe cut an album with my favorite songs.

Perhaps I'll find new adventures, like delving deeper into city building and public policy, creating a school to teach what I think is beautiful and important and right, or finding a way to bridge cultures that I love and help people understand each other. Perhaps I'll find something I haven't even thought of yet! I definitely want to find a way to give back to communities around me and help those who are struggling. I want to do my part to help repair America, the country that has blessed me with so much opportunity.

I'm grateful for the mentors in this book, who live by the light of their convictions, from whom I've learned to believe in mine. These are the unsung heroes of American business. You may never hear about them, but each day they get up and make a difference in people's lives. What I've learned from the great characters in this book is that doing something you believe in is the greatest reward. And I'm grateful for the chance to keep learning.

Real estate can be one exciting stage on which to tell your story. If your tale is one of joy and exuberance, or slow, careful progress, if it's about finding your own way on a path that others don't understand, being honorable, making something that's beautiful, or impacting people's lives in a meaningful way, there's a role to play. It's been a great journey for me and one that's still unfolding.

I hope you've found some joy and inspiration in this tale. Rest assured, you don't have to sing opera to build great real estate! You just have to find that same passion, those values, that emotional generosity and authenticity, and find a way to put it into your work. You can succeed in business with passion and honor. And if it's possible in the toughest business in the world, and in some of the toughest and most gutsy cities in the world, it's possible anywhere. This pandemic has given us the chance to think anew, and to do better. We have great buildings, flourishing neighborhoods, and a better world to build. Happy trails and God bless.

Acknowledgments

A huge thank you to my friends, family, colleagues, and mentors who have helped bring this book to fruition. To my business partners and investors, who have lived these stories with me and laughed and cried together. To my wife, who has brought love and joy to the process and juggled many responsibilities so that I could finish this meaningful work. To my parents, who have believed in me from day one, my uncles, who have been incredibly fun guides in business and life, my grandmother, who taught me to love America and its promise, and my brothers, who brought their brilliance and encouragement to various drafts of this book (not to mention my life!). A big hug and all my love and respect to each of you.

Without the tireless efforts of my editor Claire Wachtel, who believed I had this book in me somewhere, it would never have come into existence. A big shout-out to Kris Pauls and Alli Shapiro at Disruption Books and Michael Flynn at West Wing Writers for your confidence and energy. Thank you to Moshe Schulman, publicist and food and wine impresario extraordinaire, and to Jordan Fox of MMP Digital. A huge thank you to my friend Daniel Petroff, who helped me improve each draft while pursuing New York adventures.

And to the cities and country that have given me the inspiration and occasional magic to make this book a reality, my sincere appreciation and a promise to share the same kismet with the next generation.

About the Author

Joshua Benaim is a leading real estate investor and entrepreneur. He is the founder and CEO of Aria, an award-winning real estate company on a mission to humanize the experience of living in our great cities. An operatic baritone who has appeared with the Metropolitan Opera and throughout the United States, Benaim lives in New York City with his wife and three children.

⊙ @joshua_benaim

realestatealovestory.com

ariadevelopmentgroup.com

arialiving.com